Learning & Growing

A Lifetime of Service by God's Grace

by

Mrs Eunice Cynthia McGhie-Belgrave MBE

Learning and Growing. A lifetime of Service by God's Grace

Authored by Mrs Eunice Cynthia McGhie-Belgrave MBE,

with parts as told to Marcia M. Spence.

© Mrs Eunice McGhie-Belgrave MBE 2019

Cover Design Marcia M Publishing House

Photographs are the property of the author, Mrs Eunice McGhie-Belgrave MBE.

Images and press cuttings detailed on the References and Photo Credits.

Co-ordinated by Marcia M Spence, assisted by Charlene Hemans, Shelly Allmark Audrey Jackson and Olive Pellington. Edited by Susan Brookes, Lee Dickenson with Marcia M Publishing House Editorial Team. Published by Marcia M Spence of Marcia M Publishing House, West Bromwich, West Midlands the UNITED KINGDOM B71.

All rights reserved 2019 Marcia M Publishing House

Eunice McGhie-Belgrave MBE (Mrs) asserts the moral right to be identified as the author of this work.

This book is sold subject to the condition that it is not, by way of trade or otherwise, lent, hired out or otherwise circulated in any form of binding or cover other than that in which it is published. No part of this publication may be reproduced, stored in a retrieval system or transmitted in any form or by any means (electronic, mechanical, photocopying, recording or otherwise) without prior written permission from the Author or Publisher.

www.marciampublishing.com

EUNICE CYNTHIA FINLAYSON 1954

My Passport Photograph

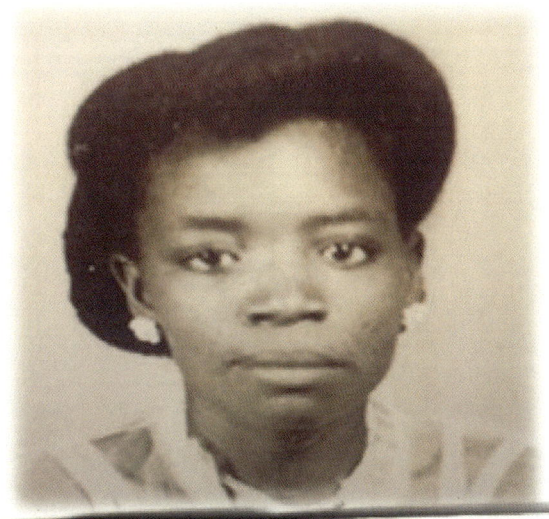

My Mother
Mrs Josephine Advira Finlayson-Thompson

My Mother, Josephine Finlayson, was a very hard-working individual. She was the youngest of her siblings and stayed at home with her mother. She was a devoted Christian..

It is important to say my Mother was worried and distressed about my birth, because that's not the way she intended her life should have been, with her first child born out of marriage. Nonetheless it happened, and the best of a bad job had to be made good, and so it was.

As her daughter whilst growing up, I had to share her grief. My Mother was very caring and loved by all.

My Mother had learnt family life is very hard to cope with; almost every family in the world has very serious problems to deal with. Therefore, my mother had done extremely well with all her children, because we all had an excellent understanding of life's journey and struggles, and we all are eternally grateful for her loving care and sustainability. She presented to us all through the struggles and respectability of life's complicated journeys may God bless her always.

Dedicated to All,
Especially to the Children

Everyone has their very own technique of educational learning experiences. I am hoping that within this written documentation all individuals will find some meaningful references within this information that will help them make the most of life's opportunities.

Acknowledgements

My Family

My Mother - Josephine Finlayson-Thompson

My Grandmother - Lea Finlayson (Leah)

Mr Chandla Davidson McGhie

Mr A McGhie – A McGhie

Mr C McGhie

Mrs B McGhie – Rhule – Ms B McGhie-Rhule and her daughter Ms Barnet

Ms L. McGhie

Mr M McGhie

Ms S McGhie

Ms P McGhie

L McGhie

Mrs M McGhie

My Community

Mrs Fozia Shahzad

Mrs S Hyman

Mr M. Tye and pupils

Head teachers in primary and secondary schools

Ministers in churches

Students in colleges and universities

Mrs Aza Parven

Mr Hasham Ulhad

THE PLOT: Eunice McGhee-Belgrave and Sonia Hyman, co-ordinators of the project, with schoolchildren.

My Grandchildren

Grandparents Inspiration

Mrs Eunice McGhie's grandson, Marcus McGhie has been a keen volunteer with the Shades of Black project committee and over the years has donated his valuable time and skills to help this project.

In January 2010, Marcus followed in his grandfather's footsteps and was enlisted into the Royal Air Force, Halton for general training. This is what Marcus had to say before he was recruited...

"My name is Marcus McGhie and I am currently a volunteer for Shades of Black, my grandmother Mrs Eunice McGhie-Belgrave MBE is the chairperson. I usually do administration work for Shades of Black but I occasionally do some video recording, photography and desktop publishing.

I went to Hamstead Hall School and achieved 9 GCSE's and then I attended Sandwell College and received my City & Guilds Electrical Installation Level 2 and Level 3 qualifications.

My grandmother inspires me a lot, especially since she was awarded her MBE in 2002 for services to the community. It's a great achievement for her. I think it's amazing that she does all this work for the local school pupils, teachers and senior citizens. That is why I try to get involved as much as possible.

It's a misfortune that I will have to give up the voluntary work when I join the RAF but I will be giving back to my country in a different way. My grandfather was in the RAF during World War II which is one of the main reasons why I am joining."

• Marcus documents one of the Shades of Black Projects.
• Marcus's grandfather during his Royal Air Force recruitment. Opposite, proud grandmother Mrs Eunice McGhie MBE with Marcus at his Pass Out Parade.

Schools Acknowledgements

15 local secondary and primary schools have participated in The Shades of Black Community Family Projects.

Handsworth Wood Girls' School

Foundary Primary and Infant School

St. John Wall Secondary RSC School

Wilkes Green Infant School

St. Augustine R.C School

Grove Lane Infant School

Stechford Primary School

Muslim/Asian primary schools

Corpus Christi Primary School

Holy Trinity secondary school

Welford School

Rookery School

Wattville School

Hamd House School

CONTENTS

Introduction 1

Chapter One: My Birth as I Was Told 5

Chapter Two: My Inspirational Family Life 13

Chapter Three: Community Action Work in Jamaica 21

Chapter Four: World War II 25

Chapter Five: My First Love 29

Chapter Six: From Paradise to Reality, 1957 33

Chapter Seven: Life in England 35

Chapter Eight: Marriage & Divorce 47

Chapter Nine: Raising My Children Alone 53

Chapter Ten: Married Life with Reginald Belgrave 61

Chapter Eleven: Cancer My Hands-on Exerience 65

Chapter Twelve: Reflection 69

Part Two 71

Introduction: Community Action Networking in England ... 71

Awards & Accolades 91

Gallery 101

Testimonials 121

Appendix 125

Appendix 2 126

Appendix 3 128

Appendix 4 .... *..129*

Appendix 5 .... *.....130*

Appendix 6.. *.....132*

**Photograph Credits and
References** .... *.....134*

Learning & Growing

A Lifetime of Service by God's Grace

by

Mrs Eunice Cynthia McGhie-Belgrave MBE

Introduction

Learning and Growing, A Lifetime of Service by God's Grace is my story of navigating the complexities of life, illustrating how I have combined my own characteristics, work ethic and Christian values to survive many struggles.

It provides an insight into how adult education and learning opportunities have provided me with knowledge and understanding, enabling me to be more positively aware of the unpredictable and extraordinary life I've lived as a black immigrant in England.

In order to be a survivor, I have been a hard-working individual. My work has captured the admiration of the wider local community, through grace, humility and by developing and presenting an essential educational, easy learning, life skills project to the broader, local multi-cultural population in Birmingham, UK, through the Shades of Black Community Family Project. It was vital my contribution and involvement were made with good knowledge at a grassroots level, with real honesty and genuine understanding for all people.

I am deeply moved by the generosity and participation of headteachers, teaching staff and pupils from local schools. My life and work have been an extraordinary and encouraging experience for me through my Christian faith. God, Our Heavenly Father, through the scriptures has supplied my daily needs, so I could serve my community alongside raising my family. This is where my Christian beliefs have excelled and exceeded all expectations.

Not only have I aided intergenerational diversity cohesion, meaning that I have brought together people of all ages,(including children and elders),races and faiths to work together, to learn and grow together. We have worked together to develop a stronger community through this unique service delivery. It is the simple things such as gardening, basic skills, hands-on learning, teaching, teamwork, a programme of activities, ideas, involvement and development that have enabled the positive achievements and consistent sustainability for participation.

A clear vision, practical and encouraging communication and leadership skills were vital. I had to be consistent and confident when speaking in order to encourage community involvement and inspire others.

I have utilised skills, knowledge, personality traits and characteristics, which I inherited from my parents, and developed myself, to my full potential, enabling me to make a difference to thousands of individuals.

This book is about my own challenges, struggles, survival, and achievements from 1934 to 2019. I've worked hard from a young age and continue to do so even in my 5 years80s. Any opinions expressed in these pages are my own and should not be associated with any of the individuals mentioned in the acknowledgements.

It has taken eight years of hard work to complete this book, and I am grateful for the love and devotion of others.

May I take this opportunity to extend my thanks to all for your invaluable assistance through what I have embraced as the remarkable and extraordinary journey of my life. I hope you will find inspiration, wisdom and knowledge of educational learning within these pages.

Eunice

Mrs Eunice Cynthia McGhie--Belgrave MBE

Mrs Eunice Cynthia McGhie-Belgrave MBE

Father Me
(O Father of the Fatherless)

by Graham Kendrick

O Father of the fatherless
in whom all families are blessed
I love the way You father me
You gave me life, forgave the past
now in Your arms I"m safe at last
I love the way You father me

Father me, forever You"ll father me
and in Your embrace I"ll be forever secure
I love the way You father me
I love the way You father me

When bruised and broken I draw near
You hold me close and dry my tears
I love the way You father me
At last my fearful heart is still
surrendered to Your perfect will
I love the way You father me

If in my foolishness I stray
returning empty and ashamed
I love the way You father me
Exchanging for my wretchedness
Your radiant robes of righteousness
I love the way You father me

And when I look into Your eyes
from deep within my spirit cries
I love the way You father me
Before such love I stand amazed
and ever will through endless days
I love the way You father me
© 1992 Make Way Music

Chapter One

"Illegitimacy was frowned upon, it was hidden; grandparents would take the child on because it was frowned upon, because it was the English law."

My Birth as I Was Told...

I was born on the 11th of October 1934. My birthplace was on the Caribbean island of Jamaica in the Parish of St James Maldon District in the countryside. In 1934, it was part of the Commonwealth ruled by the British Empire.

At the age of seven, my grandmother, Leah Finlayson thought it was wisdom to start a converstion about my birth. She was one of the local midwives for the whole of the Maldon District. Grandmother Leah was a fully-fledged Christian, and she was humble, full of humanity, empathy, kindness and compassion. Grandmother was graceful, tolerant and kind-hearted to anyone who met her and her family, husband, five children: Aunt Birdie, Reginald, Uncle Brother, Uncle Smith and my Mother, who was the youngest of the five children.

My Grandmother Leah made her home a communal setting open to local people near and far. She also encouraged her sister-in-law and others to find professional work within and around the area where we lived. Grandma Leah was an enabler; she was interested in education and progression.

My grandmother's story of human conscience and kindness for the poor in the wider community benefitted others. In my grandmother's day, she worked tirelessly to serve the local community. At the age of 95 years she began to show signs of ill health, and her daughter nursed her until her death at 97 years old in the 1980s. In her nursing career, she always cared for the local community and continuously built bridges and supplied specialist care for new-born babies. Grandmother witnessed disastrous conditions which were devastating. This is where determination, hard work, obedience and an excellent attitude towards life's journeys can be assured, despite the struggles foreseen and told.

My childhood was good. I was happy living with my mother and grandmother. My grandmother, Leah Finlayson, thought it was wise to talk constructively about my conception and birth.

The rivalry and jealousy between families and non-family members all over the world are inevitable and devastating. The problems highlighted in my conception were instigated by her older sister, who was married with four children, during the time my mother was living at home with her mother.

My mother was locked in a room with my father by her married sister whilst her mother was out delivering other families' children. This is what I was told happened; that's why my mother was devastated.

Josephine Advira Finlayson, a slender, caramel black woman, like grandad with long flowing locks of wavy hair, and my father Hilton Morris, were Christians brought up in the church. Christianity didn't condone sex outside marriage. When this pair met, they developed a relationship and were deeply in love, but when her sister locked them in that room, I cannot say that my father was as committed a Christian as my mother was.

To be told how my mother had been treated by my father after and his family after conception was very humiliating and frustrating for me. I was at the age of seven years, when morals can only just be understood by a child. I was told they were in love with each other, both were sexually attracted to each other and when locked in that room together they tried the process of love-making but had not thought about the repercussions of conceiving and having a child as an unmarried couple.

Babies born out of wedlock were a huge source of shame to all communities in the 1930s, especially a Christian family. These types of pregnancies would precipitate a fast wedding arrangement or some social exclusion and stigma for the unmarried mother, her family and her child. Immediately after the pregnancy was made public, my father was sent away to the capital city Kingston to seek employment and told by his family never to return.

This left my mother and the Finlayson family in a distressed state and gave the church community an ethical dilemma, as my grandmother had a high position in church life. My grandmother could continue her church position, her midwife work and to care for her daughter, because she and the family were so respected. She also continued to help other local people.

I loved my mother dearly: no one could and would be able to separate us from each other, even when we were thousands of miles away in England. I had a letter every month from her until death. My beloved mother's letters are in my historical documentation at the museum in Birmingham city centre.

In life and death there are struggles to face, so let's be kind and considerate to our mothers, who brought us life to live, and love. I thank God for my mother every day of my life; we have all made mistakes in our lives.

The stories behind my unpredictable and extraordinary life have been a reality which needs to be shared through my solid personal faith in the Lord God Almighty, the Creator.

My mother faced the months of pregnancy alone whilst nursing a broken heart, as she loved Hilton. The distress felt during my mother's pregnancy led to my premature birth.

I was delivered by grandmother Finlayson. I think I was born about six weeks before I was due. My mom was very distressed in her pregnancy. For nearly a year I was placed on specially-made pillows, because I was tiny. In those days, medical aid was scarce. One had to travel a long way to find doctors and chemists within rural areas, so we didn't really have that type of care close to us. It was very reassuring that my grandmother was well trained in her profession. She also had a brother who was a doctor, and they helped her when she needed any medical advice. Their advice was necessary for my survival and thousands of others.

In England and Jamaica, because of the rules and laws set down in the years of the Empire, a young woman and man had to be married to have children, otherwise they were discredited. Some chose to hide the pregnancy or give away their children to different people to bring them up across the generations.

There were a large number of blacks that would not have had any education before and after 1930 because of the racism and slavery by white cultivation landowners in Jamaica and across the world.

My family and I are always very considerate towards all individuals who are not able to be educated and we tried our best to assist in every way possible. Many of our parents have not been taught to sit with their children, to educate them about sexual matters, because they themselves felt ill-equipped to have those conversations with their children.

It was certainly not considered an appropriate way of life to live with partners without being husband and wife. Parents had to be responsible when living with children and set a standard as law-abiding citizens, and this had to be maintained in the 1930s.

Education, along with excellent knowledge and understanding, are vital resources to succeed in every situation. Not every individual has the opportunity to prepare themselves for their future or obtain these opportunities in their lifetime.

I was brought up by the Finlayson family in my grandmother's home, where both my mother and I lived from my birth. The house was six rooms with a big room, a dining room and lounge for visitors, and lots of land. I slept with mom in one of the bedrooms, but I could also sleep with grandma, and I often did under her arm, or I could use my own bed too. My grandma made all our clothes, everything for everybody, and my uncle made me a toy sewing machine.

Grandma loved children so much, she would make clothes for them to wear from any materials they could afford, just to help the poor survive. She taught children from three to five years of age how to enjoy learning methods in a constructive and straightforward manner, with heartfelt love and devotion. Being very spiritual, this was my grandmother's specialist subject. She got the children to memorise the Lord's Prayer, Psalm 23, the Ten Commandments and other scripture passages, as well as teaching them times tables and to count to 100 before they reached school age. This was an excellent way to kickstart the educational journey of both disadvantaged and able-bodied young children. She used structured planning to make learning easy and suitable for all. My grandmother assisted her children's, grandchildren's and the wider community's education and welfare. My communication skills were made to develop very early, at three years of age. I was on stage in church through Sunday school teachers, reading or reciting short scripture verses from the Holy Bible. This is what my parents and church members, as well as the wider community, had encouraged us to do.

The Morris family believed their son had to marry my mother, which was a common belief in those days. They sent him to find work and he was expected to return, but he never came back.

It was surprising that when I reached 11 years of age, I received a birthday card in the post from my father. It was nice to receive this from him at that time. That was the only time I heard from him when I was growing up.

I wasn't adversely affected by not having my father or his family around, because I was well looked after by my mother, grandmother, uncles, aunts and the local extended church family. My memories are happy ones. There was little doubt about their ability to care for me, because they were loved so much by the extended family and the wider community.

Mother and grandmother were my parents because there was not a father present until my stepfather married my mother. I had two brothers and two sisters.

Fathers are as important as mothers in their children's well-being, but sometimes it is not possible for them to be around. It's essential for a child to know their father if their father wants to know them. That is the other question; does their father want to know them? Some men will have children all over the world because they think it is the thing to do. But they are not prepared to take responsibility.

When I embarked on my epic journey to England, I had no idea that the same conflicts about absent parents, especially fatherless children, would reoccur. It just shows that all nations of the world have these hidden complexities and struggles within life's journey.

I often think the Baptist Church song of the spirit, *O Father of the Fatherless*, enables struggles to be more easily handled. It contains such beautiful words. It is through

God's mercy, a lot of prayers and making sure that I understood what I had to do, that I have been able to carry on. Even my schoolfriends in Jamaica, if they were alive to talk to you, would say, "she never say much." I told them nothing about my personal life.

I was well protected because of the way my grandmother and mother had assisted my understanding and because I was always a bright, intelligent child. I went to all the mayors' houses; all the kids and I slept in their houses at night. I used to look after the minister's children because I could read and write. I used to read for families in their homes, and I would read for individuals who were lawyers and, because of that sort of assistance, I used to earn quite a bit of finance. I started when I was about eight years old.

My life might have been different if I had been raised by my father but I cannot say that it would have been better. Every individual has a life story, but they will only talk, or document this, when they have to, or when the time is right to do so. It should be done with honesty and pride. My concern is about our future generations of children; I hope they may be inspired to learn well, so they too will be inspirational to others.

Learning and Growing. A lifetime of Service by God's Grace

Chapter Two

"I had an excellent upbringing."

My Inspirational Family Life

As I've said previously, I was born in the countryside, in the Parish of St James, in the district of Maldon, Jamaica. This was part of the British Empire, but poverty was prevalent, especially amongst black people.

My grandfather and grandmother were heads of the household and believed in doing what was right in the sight of God. Grandmother always upheld her caring duty and bestowed it on everyone equally. Being born between two world wars and where poverty existed meant families had to share what they had with each other and be comfortable, honest and hard-working to earn a living.

Grandmother and mother cared about their sons, daughters and grandchildren, and gave them unconditional love and understanding. They helped us develop many skills in our early years, such as reading, writing, sewing, cooking, fieldwork (farm work) and timekeeping. Each aspect was necessary, and time was spent on each subject individually. They planned each day so that it provided an essential elementary guide to life's learnings, expectations and experiences.

I learnt about public speaking through the Holy Bible verses or from English elementary school literature books. Books read included *Hiawatha, King Arthur and several others.*

Before five years of age, from within a caring family home and through Sunday school teaching, most children were supervised by their parents to read, write, learn times tables and maths. Games were also played, around the maypole, tee ta toe, marbles, catapult slings, cricket, ball games. This would enable children to settle into the school environment when they started in 1939.

In school, most of the teachers were from England and other overseas countries. Whilst training was made available to black students, their study work was sent to England for marking and results. Without having signed recognition documentation from England, teachers would not be qualified in their professional teaching careers.

Falling in love with learning is a beautiful concept to follow because it does not become hard labour, but a labour of love. Planning and excellent communication play essential parts in easy, concentrated learning, although quite a few individuals find learning very difficult in organised spaces. Therefore I am so thankful and grateful to my family, who taught me these simple, basic skills of easy learning.

My school life was easy and I did well with my teachers, I reached a high standard because the early years education with grandmother, mother and the extended family unit was excellent. I excelled and was praised for the work I did in school from five to 14 years old. I was granted two years further study in recognition of my hard work and immaculate attendance, despite coming from a poor background. I found it a wonderful and enjoyable experience.

Born without a father to converse with, I found living with my grandmother, mother and other immediate family members a beautiful and exceptional experience. The fascination was about order, honesty, hard work, obedience and unconditional love, which existed through the life lived and practiced throughout my 22 years four months in Jamaica that developed and enabled 63 years of life in England.

I was taught many poems and recitations when I was in school, and this one I genuinely believe in. I have lived by this throughout my life. I remember it from my childhood days as clearly as the first day I heard it. That was the way that we were taught in school in Jamaica in the 1930s: English literature, the classics, and we had to read and recite them.

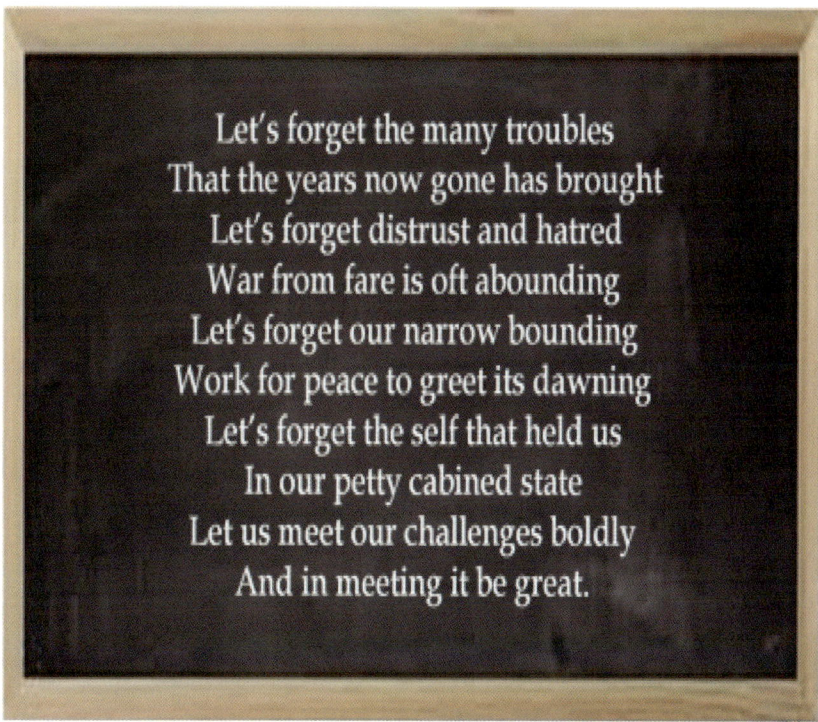

> Let's forget the many troubles
> That the years now gone has brought
> Let's forget distrust and hatred
> War from fare is oft abounding
> Let's forget our narrow bounding
> Work for peace to greet its dawning
> Let's forget the self that held us
> In our petty cabined state
> Let us meet our challenges boldly
> And in meeting it be great.

I remember that I, my grandmother, mother and sometimes other family members would walk for two-and-a-half miles in the morning, leaving home at 8 a.m. for the start of lessons at 8.45 a.m. and we did this again when lessons finished at 3.30 p.m. That was until we were old enough to make the journey just with the help of our friends and siblings.

Before going to school in the morning, household chores or farm work had to be done, and we had to be ready in smart uniforms of navy blue pleated skirts, navy blue tie, black shoes or black pumps, navy bags with books, pencil and whatever was affordable for lunch. After school before doing any other duties, our shoes had to be polished and our uniform had to be ironed, so that we would be ready for school the next day.

On Saturdays, after selling our farm produce in the market, we played games. Sundays revolved around church life. Parents joined in activities such as singing, drama, preaching and cookery. Sunday school catered for children of different ages. A wonderful time was had by all.

The natural, changeable weather conditions were enjoyable, but when heavy storms and earthquakes happened, the living conditions in Jamaica were severely interrupted, and sometimes houses had to be rebuilt.

Mother found love again with Mr Clifford Thompson. My stepfather was a very quiet and reserved individual. He was hard-working. They married when I was about three years of age. They had four children, two girls and two boys, and although her husband had a home, she stayed in her mother's house for many years. We were all raised together by our mother and grandmother.

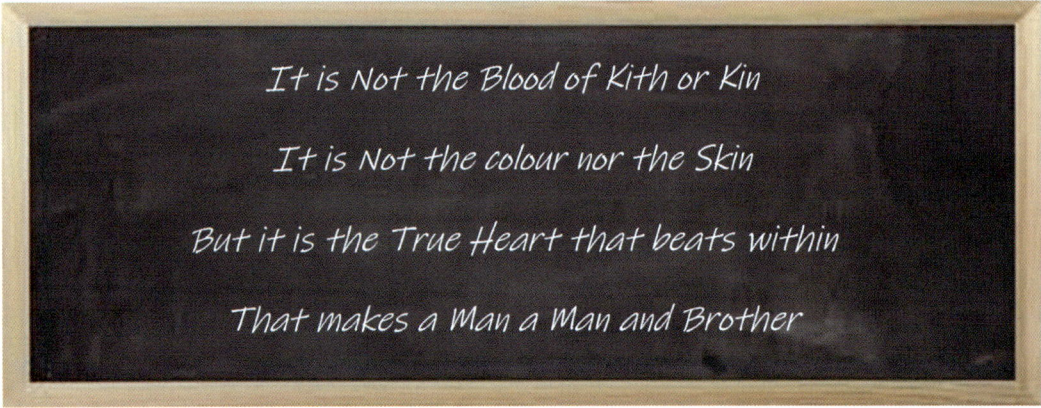

It is Not the Blood of Kith or Kin

It is Not the colour nor the Skin

But it is the True Heart that beats within

That makes a Man a Man and Brother

To complete school and teenage years with brothers and sisters makes it an all-round lifestyle without personal father insight.

It would be complex to try to differentiate between my father and stepfather, because I spent very little time in their presence. I loved mother dearly, but I was never close to my stepfather because it was mother, grandmother and uncles that were responsible for my parental care and, together, they fulfilled my needs.

The little time spent with my stepfather showed he was motivated most of the time. He was hard-working and had a beautiful voice in song, and so did mother. What I remember most is on Sunday evenings, after church services, he entertained us with his beautiful singing voice. When mother joined in, we could have sat and listened for hours. The local community also loved them both dearly. People used to come and listen to them sing and play music; they entertained. My whole family can sing; they have good voices and I like to sing too. It was great.

As he was not my real father, we had very little in common, but I respected him as my mother's husband. He did not interfere between me and mother. He had a kind heart and was loved by the local community. I also believe for any man to bear the burden of fatherhood of another man's child would be a very terrible strain and injustice if it is not done of free will.

My stepfather lived with his mother for many years, but when she died, my mother moved to live with him, but I stayed with my grandmother.

At the age of seven I began a job after school, reading the editorial page of the newspaper to a lady who was a secretary in the law courts so she could improve her shorthand and typing skills. I did this in her home. The money I earned went towards the family budget.

At the age of ten, my evenings were divided between reading, looking after the pastor's children and studying.

Remember my father sent me a birthday card when I was 11 years of age, and it was 11 years and four months after the birthday card that we met face to face along with his family. The meeting was strange, with very little emotion, but at least he had fulfilled his longing for a face to face meeting. He told me the same as what my grandmother had said, that it was his mother who had caused the split between him and my mother. He told me he regretted that it had happen, but he had not had the courage to be strong for himself. We have never met again. I have never had a photo of my father. I have also learnt that I am not the only child to have never had the opportunities of these memorable chances and moments in life's journey and experiences.

I have no bitterness towards my father; I had an unusually positive parental upbringing in parts, especially in lessons of both basic skills and academic education. Giving me a collective forward knowledge and understanding towards life's epic journey of successful achievements, and also struggles each individual has to face with positive determination to overcome adversities.

To have scored points between two parents living hundreds of miles apart would not have been honourable. I always keep being positive and truthful to myself and others. My advice to many is to be healthy and work hard.

My teenage years were challenging. I had to maintain the standards set by my family. I wanted to do some of the things that my parents prevented me from doing. I wanted to sometimes go out late like the others, but I wouldn't do that. Once, my schoolfriend Isolyn and I walked together to a Seventh Day Adventist church service. Whilst we were there, some lads invited her to go out with them. When the service finished, I had to walk home alone. The first thing I heard in the morning was that she had been raped by seven men. These incidents seem to happen all over the world, but when you are young it's very difficult to understand.

Isolyn's reputation was tarnished. If I had followed her that night I would have been in the same position. It's not good to follow others, but I was protected because I listened to my parents. Ostracised from the community; she told me she wished she had stayed with me in the church meeting.

I experienced changeable emotions thinking about the complexities of life. I didn't talk much but would listen to people speaking. I had my teachings from my grandmother, but other people's perspectives were different from my upbringing.

I asked grandmother and mother difficult questions about the facts of life, sexual problems and personal, intimate and delicate matters I was concerned and confused about. I would hear young people talking about sex and I was puzzled. Sexual problems can be caused by misunderstanding in intimate and delicate matters of concern.

A lot of young people were having sex and talking about how, where and what to do. There were a lot of uneducated young people talking about sex and intimate relationships in those days. It was not as coarse as today. I asked my parents, but if they did not want to tell me about something, they would say they'd tell me later. The older generation didn't like it when children asked questions, and said it wasn't the right time. That was the etiquette then.

At 16 years of age I had a period of unexplained illness for several months whilst working away from home. I was working in Trelawny in a shop, so I had to sleep on the premises. One night I heard banging and knocking halfway through the night. I opened the door and from that moment I was ill.

I was in bed for months. I had a fever and was shaking and my mom and grandma couldn't understand it. My aunts and other members of the family did not help. In a dream I met Jesus, and when I looked towards the skies, I saw two white doves bowing down to each other. After this, Jesus appeared as He's seen in photographs. He seemed to stand still and then gently fade away. From that night onwards I knew that there was no escape from a spiritual lifestyle.

But it was in England, with daughter Bernadette in 1988, that a public commitment was confirmed by my under-water baptism because, in my heart, the time was right for a life-long, unbroken and unconditional commitment to the Lord. Christianity makes provision through an inner strength which helps cope with life's struggles through prayer responses, and makes life more understandable through Holy Bible readings. This is about making the right choice, which shall always be yours and yours alone

After recovery from my sudden illness, I was ready to be working again. I went off to Montego Bay to find work. I found that working hard is always the best option for survival and staying focused. As a young teen growing up in Maldon, it was very nice to know that community people had recognised the work done by teenagers, after finishing school. It was nice to know that, through multi-tasking work learnt through school education and parent intervention, finance could be earned. Domestic work would belittle many people, but cleanliness is next to Godliness.

Mother and grandmother's families were extraordinary within the community of Maldon. We were all Christian-led, everyone showed respect and our house was very open to visitors and local community people; nothing seemed impossible no matter how difficult. Whenever there was a dispute to settle, everyone had to join in a place or grandmother would not interfere. Thank God for grandmother Leah, who lived and died at 97 years of age in the 1900s. Mother died in the late-1980s.

Jamaican Coat of Arms

Chapter Three

Community Action Work in Jamaica

I did a variety of jobs in Jamaica before arriving in England. My family encouraged this in my teenage years to help me develop and gain resilience and great understanding.

There was always uncertainty that travelling overseas may not happen, but it was always promoted as something that would be worth its weight in gold. Talk of this assisted me to forward plan in a very positive way.

To be hard-working in whatever job you are set, whether this becomes your career or not, is very important, as it is helpful to have a positive attitude. At home in Jamaica, work was and is still tough.

Working in sugar fields, cutting canes and in cane-grinding mills, growing and picking coffee beans, farmwork, dressmaking, crocheting, cooking for your family or providing services to the rich, working in a shop, or undertaking road repairs, all of these jobs are hard work.

Many also take place in poor environmental working conditions and inadequate management. They are accompanied by the hot sun, heavy rains or earthquakes, which cause ruin and lead to the need for rubble clearing and starting all over, again and again. This work needs positive action to be accomplished.

The way a parent trains their child is important. It takes time to teach them how to follow instructions and to answer their questions in a positive and straightforward manner. Children should always be taught to be humble and to have a good attitude and work hard to achieve excellent results with deep satisfaction. Almost all children are very intelligent, and with help from their parents, they will be inspired to achieve their goals, meet any changes, struggles and discoveries on life's journey.

Water Access in Rural Areas of Jamaica

In the capital city in Jamaica, there were water tanks and standpipes in some homes. There were also standpipes at the end of long streets. In the rural countryside, standpipes are available within a three-mile radius, although not in all places. In order to have the use of water from the standpipes, everyone in the family at some time had to fetch water by carrying large containers on their heads, using protection to prevent damaging the skull. Water was also obtained from rivers, caves and rainfall, collected in large barrels, oil drums or clay pots.

Cultivation in Rural Areas/Sales in the Capital City and School

When I was growing up in the rural areas of Jamaica, country life was very hard. Individuals and families had to work on farms for low wages and sometimes exchange labour of one sort or another as part of each settlement. Small farms are the norm and produce crops to be harvested to feed the family, with some surplus for sale in the large city markets. This income makes a real difference to the quality of life. The produce is carried in baskets on individual's heads or by donkey or mule to the market place. Livestock is taken in trucks. It is always the responsibility of the buyers to arrange transport for their purchases e.g. yams, bananas, sweet potatoes, bread, fruits, sugar canes, coconuts and others such as herbs, vegetables and flowers.

In every country around the world, not every individual or family is the same. There are poor and there are poorer. Education matters, be it basic skills or higher academia. The children, pupils, students and families who were obedient to their parents, teachers and educational studies always strived towards the best that could be obtained in education in the period 1900-1950, when life in the West Indies was a struggle for all. Jamaica was not the only country experiencing a hard time. It seemed to be a global phenomenon throughout the whole world.

In Jamaica, we had white plantation and cultivation owners who exploited black workers sexually, through slavery and by racism. The product of this was the families created with one white and one black parent. My own grandmother was a white plantation owners daughter.

It was through this channel of workers cultivating sugar cane, banana plantations, cocoa and coffee beans, and through domestic workers and those working in other situations, that racism was commonplace for thousands of Jamaicans. Workers were exploited by white plantation and cultivation owners from all over the world. In almost every struggle and challenge, one can find a reasonable individual who offers help. So, I personally would say there is always one white individual whose inward conscience would persuade him or her to be more helpful to others. Without that life-changing decisive action, nothing would change. Thank God for those who will. My question is, why did white people hate black people so much? We all have red blood in our DNA. I would love an answer please.

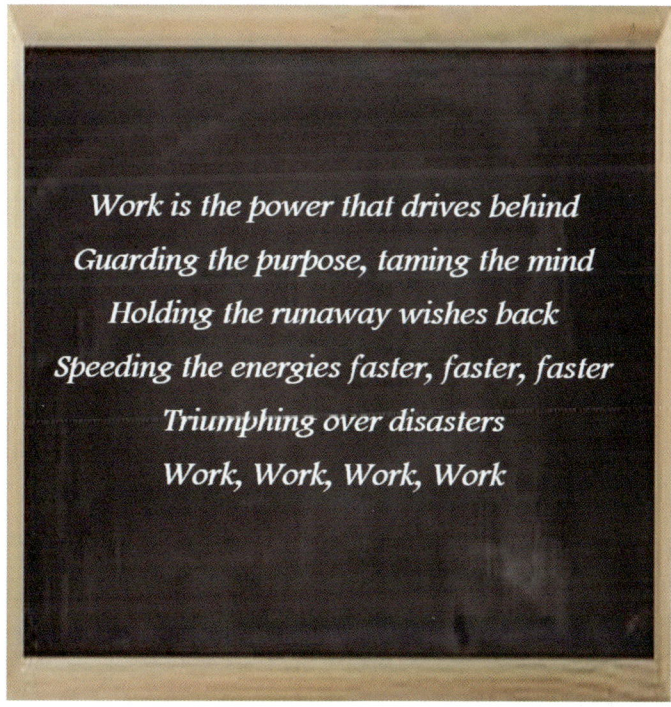

Another poem from my childhood

Jamaican Airman World War II

Chapter Four

World War II

During World War II, a high number of young men and woman aged 16-20 from the West Indies were recruited to assist in the war effort in England. As Jamaica was part of the British Empire, the government couldn't refuse. It was through these circumstances that Mr Roland Finlayson and Mr Chandla Davidson McGhie and thousands of others were recruited and trained for three months in Jamaica. They travelled to England by ship to work on their allocated tasks, and told their stories through letters and verbal communication on their return after the war in 1949.

After the war, most soldiers returned home bruised and unhealthy because of the traumas of World War II. Some, like Chandla, were better than others and wanted to return to England. On his departure in 1955, he had promised to pay my airfare as soon as possible for the journey of a lifetime, as our love had blossomed.

I had heard how living in England would be very difficult because of the racism encountered, and reaction to reflection on black immigrants by white people in England because of the colour of your skin.

I was only five years old in 1939 when World War II began. It was in 1944, at nine years of age, that the reality of war was evident to everyone. The real horror of World War II was highlighted as the recruitment into the forces of young men and women at the age of eighteen and nineteen was commonplace.

Daily life went on, but poverty was always at the forefront of our lives. This is my memory of how it was then.

Imported goods from other countries e.g., America, Canada, England and several others, were in short supply. Shops were empty and this was happening all over the world. My uncle and his friends were recruited as soldiers in the Royal Air Force in 1944 and went to England in 1945 for two to five years.

During the war years, everyone had to be self-reliant. They had farms with cows, pigs and chickens and cultivated fresh vegetables to feed the population, who were living in poverty during these troubled years. My family and others did the same; people were amiable and understanding. Everyone admired the soldiers' beautiful blue uniforms, their berets, belts, shoes and accessories.

The conflicts of World War II brought death and illness and men and woman of all nationalities paid with their lives. Many of the young men and woman who'd been recruited were returned to Jamaica dead, such are the atrocities of war.

My grandmother and her sister-in-law were midwives during this historical period and would have been the very people who had brought some of those who were killed, or their family members, into this world at birth.

I can remember clearly that when the soldiers returned for leave, they always assembled at grandmother's house. I saw a lot of cameras and musical instruments. The instrument I liked best was the accordion and the songs playing on the gramophone. Kerosene oil for table lamps, petrol for cars, cloth for making garments, books, salted fish and meat, flour, rice and educational materials were all imported, but during the war years they were practically non-existent. When goods arrived occasionally by ship, they were rationed.

My parents had to gather and grate coconuts to produce oil to burn for lighting indoors at night, or we had to depend on the light from the moon during the war years. Jamaicans were visited by soldiers from across the world: the Americans, English, Irish, Africans, Chinese, Japanese and others.

The Zeppelin aeroplanes also came to drop bombs. Everyone was frightened, and movement was restricted, especially at night, when all the windows and doors had to be lined with whatever was available at the time. The capital cities were in danger, the enemies were everywhere. It was then that double windows were created so that no lights could be seen by the enemies.

In the Caribbean, we too had near misses from bombs. It was Christianity and the church assembly that played a crucial role in binding us together to live as the Creator commands. God Lord Jesus was the centre of our lives; people prayed and sang songs harder than ever before.

When the radio news came that World War II had ended, it was a moment of joyous celebration. Then the hard work of rebuilding communities and nations worldwide began.

After reading this brief account of what I have seen and heard, you will understand why I have an interest in World War II stories.

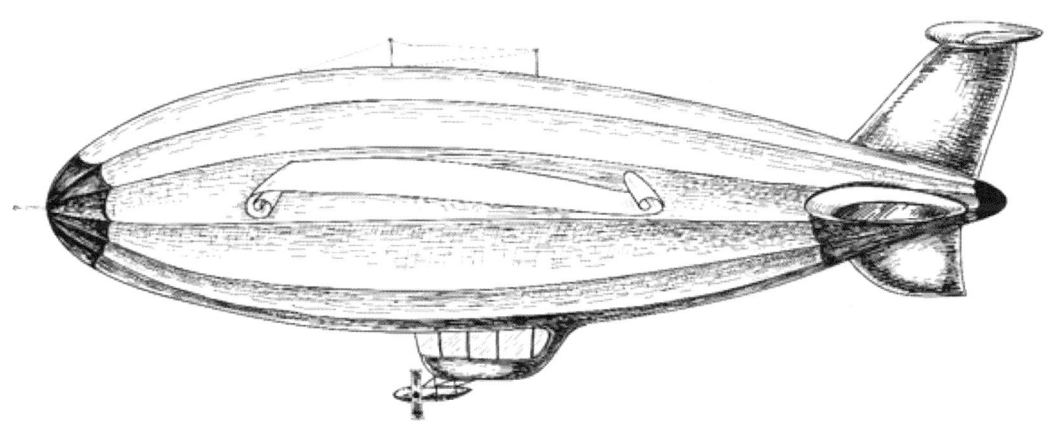

Zeppelin Aircraft

Chapter Five

My First Love

My first loving encounter was with ex-soldier Mr Chandla McGhie at the tender age of 17, on his return from England in the 1950s, in the presence of my

My First Husband Chandla McGhie

mother. He watched me growing up at my grandmother's home, where he often came to visit my uncle, who was also in the Royal Air Force.

So, what happened was, Chandla and my uncle and some other men recruited to the Royal Air Force would return to Jamaica for rest periods on holidays. Because of the way grandma treated the whole community, It was an open home, the heart of the community. The men would gather there and listen to and talk about music; that's how my first love saw me grow up. Then when he returned from the war years he still came to our home and talked to my mother about us getting together.

The first time we met was in Maroon town, in the District Saint James Parish of Jamaica, where he lived with his immediate family; his mother, father and sister. This was not very far from the centre, where all essential services such as a health clinic, doctor's surgery, dental service, post office and several other amenities were placed. As it was in the 1950s, all parents were involved in their children's social and private affairs, so it was during a conversation with my mother that he made his intentions towards me very clear.

He said he would like to visit my home because he would like me to be friends with him. In those days you would have to talk to the parents about it. As was the practice in the 1950s, a formal verbal invitation was given by my mother for Chandla to attend our family home, and he accepted.

On arrival he was met by my mother and my grandmother, and both discussed with him, in-depth, what may and may not happen in my future. They clearly all reached an agreement and mutual understanding about the traditional aspect of a respectful, long-term love, romance and marriage. I was then asked to join in the conversation.

He was older than me. I was about 18 or something like that when grandma set the rules about our courtship. I was delighted with the arrangements made on my behalf, and the emphasis on family rules and regulations and the reflection of our Christian lifestyle. This was a chance meeting where love blossomed instantly.

Then, privately, they went off and did some more talking. When they came back, they called me in and grandmother repeated what he said and then she asked, "Are you sure you understand about married life, as it will present an completely new lifestyle for you, as you both live together?"

Remember, my grandmother Leah Finlayson was a white woman who had married a black man; she knew all about the disrespect attached to these conditions and was trying to make sure both of us understood what discrimintiaon and racism was all about.

The only time I was left alone with Chandla was when he was returning to England. He took me to Montego Bay and I spent a couple of days with him in a hotel, (this was my first sexual experience), all had to be agreed with each of our parents in advance. Chandla assured my parents that when he went back to England, he was going to send for me to join him, he understood his obligation. My grandmother said, "you make sure you don't leave her with any worries!" (which meant no pregnancy). Of course, one couldn't talk about those things explicitly.

Chandla also spoke to me about his intentions. We found out in conversation that we are both Libran star sign; maybe that was the attraction. The process continued, as was customary. I was also invited by Chandla to his family home, and met his parents and other family members. I was delightfully accepted by them and made several further visits. His mother spoke to me in-depth, about being a wife and the facts of married life, as my mother had spoken to him. The love between Chandla and I continued to grow. Chandla's parents died, and he decided to travel back to England in 1955. On his departure, he had made a promise to my mother that I would follow him to England.

After two-and-a-half years of waiting, the promised dream materialised and the journey was organised with the appropriate references and all the necessary documents and arrangements made. With family, friends and community well-wishers, the journey started with prayers, fasting and saying our goodbyes on December 31st, 1956.

On January 1st 1957, my incredible epic journey of a lifetime began, and I had high expectations. I travelled by Royal Mail van to the railway station for the first part of my journey at Cambridge train station to Kingston, Jamaica.

Bamboo Walk, Jamaica

Chapter Six

From Paradise to Reality, 1957

I travelled by rail to Kingston, where arrangements had been made by Chandla to have one month's holiday from January-February 1957 before our trip to England. This was for traditional purposes. His aunty gave her nephew information about the suitability of marriage and the responsibilities of family life. There was no expectation of failure because the Christian life and family structure are very respectful, honest and hard-working. Responsibilities are firmly structured in domestic (household) management and educational basic life skills teaching and learning, especially in a poor family life setting.

It was during this holiday time in Kingston that I met my real father and his family for the first time. He seemed pleasantly surprised to see me and complimented me on my educational achievement. He told me he knew I was highly thought of by the local community and local schools and churches. His mother would have told him this. I have never seen him again. He told the same stories of my conception my parents had told me about. It's always difficult to imagine the everyday struggles and complexities of families' concerns and approaches about issues during their life's journey.

After my month's holiday, on February 8th I went in a taxi to Kingston Airport. I checked in at the departure lounge and was escorted to the aeroplane, where comfortable seats were provided. I can remember most of it. The journey started off as a joyous trip and then it became darker because I was thinking about leaving my family to come to England, and I didn't know how I was going settle. When the plane took off, I just said to myself, 'Here we go, my life is changing'. As the plane went up, I thought about missing my mother, my grandmother, all the people I knew, and about my new life and wondered, 'where am I going?' So, my mood changed and I became a little bit sad.

I belted up, ready for the next stage of the epic journey of a lifetime with mixed emotions and high expectations. As the aeroplane lifted off into the sky, riding the clouds, the thought of country life and the order, respect, discipline and care which manifested was fondly remembered. It is always the sustainable, loving, caring involvement for all human beings that teaches us about life journeys and enriches the rural individuals' lifestyle. I reflected on this during my journey. It has to be said that not everyone has these committed values and are Christian-minded but, through necessary skills educational learning programmes, working together promotes consistency and excellent communication, which has made a difference and changed lives for thousands of individuals, just like myself.

There were approximately 250 passengers on the flight to England. The aircrew carried out their hospitality duties and we stopped for scheduled refuelling in two places, Nassau in the West Indies and the Newfoundland airport in Canada.

It was my first experience of snow and an abundance of snow was pouring down. When we landed in Newfoundland for refuelling, the plane couldn't leave. It was there for two or three days, they kept changing and clearing the pathway and getting ready to fly. So, I just said to myself, 'Oh dear, if Newfoundland is like this, what is England like, what's going to happen there?" This gave me some insight, because I understood England's weather conditions to be similar to Canada's, and a potential hazard to human life.

Chapter Seven

Life in England

I arrived in England on a cold, foggy and frosty day. Here, a new life began with struggles and challenges to overcome. I wore a suit, the top was a blouse and the skirt was navy blue and black. I loved high heels, I wore black high heels and I was quite well presented. It was the only flight I have ever flown in my lifetime.

When we reached London airport the weather was the same as Newfoundland airport because it was a bad winter that year. Seeing all the snow and fog was remarkable. All the chimneys were burning, and you couldn't see yourself because of the smog. It was treacherous because of the state of the runway, we were terrified when landing in London.

My husband-to-be didn't come to meet me because he was at work, but he sent someone to meet me with a coat, thankfully , I was privileged compared to others who were left to experience the British climate, without warm enough clothing.

My family and friends were all concerned about me coming to England, like any other family. In England, racism was rife and the challenges and struggles ready to erupt as black individuals arrived.

The unpleasantness of the white population was everywhere to be seen and heard: "No Irish, No Blacks and No dogs" read a now-infamous sign.

In 1957, everyday life in Britain was an enormous struggle. Most of the difficulties were due to racism and white English individuals who didn't want to rent rooms or houses to black people. The first place we lived in was in Handsworth and it was a room that was divided by a heavy curtain. The cost of renting accommodation was £1.25 if you were single and £2.00 for couples. It was not suitable for a couple to live in. In one room which was split in half by a heavy curtain and one couple lived on the left side of the curtain and another couple on the right.

'Oh dear!' I thought to myself 'this is not good.' I could not believe it and said to my husband: "No man, I'm not living in this house." I started to make a fuss with my husband. 'After all he knew, when I was supposed to be coming, I was supposed to be getting a room, not sharing'.

We couldn't talk to one another, because of the other couple living on the other side of the room, So, soon enough, I pleaded with my husband, "you need to find another room, or I want to go back home!"

The other couple were out in the day because they had work to do. This meant Chandla and I had some privacy in the day when he was off work. So, our typical time for romance and intimacy was mostly daytime. We heard the other couple all the time and the first thing that came into my head was, 'mother and grandmother would be shocked by this'. I was used to my space at home in Jamaica so, to come into these unforeseeable conditions that I would never have chosen if I knew. So, we started looking around for our own rooms which we eventually found but we were living in rooms until I had my first son, It was after our son was born that I insisted that we buy a house or I would go back to my family and our beautiful home in Jamaica.

We lived and remained in Handsworth, we didn't move from Handsworth for many, many years. I'm not a person that moves about. There were a lot of black individuals in Handsworth, and we couldn't congregate together because of racism. You couldn't go into a pub and buy drinks and sit down; you knew the landlords and patrons wouldn't allow it.

If black people wanted to gather together, they had to have a little private party in the house. We were not accepted in the churches or public spaces because of the blatant racism that was manifesting itself all over England, and still is even if not as blatant.

Some of the other black people were not what I would call "nice-living" people either, they were different to me and my husband; we have different standards and I was a Christian. Some said I was like a white person because I was, well-spoken, I was calm and disciplined, I wasn't jumping around and loud. They would say, "you're white."

My husband was very light-skinned, so that was another thing for them to judge us with, but, I didn't let it affect me, I thought, 'well, I'm getting on with it, I will take no notice.'

They didn't like it when I placed rules and boundaries on the children and they said, "you think you're white, you think you're white."

I said, "I don't think I'm white, I'm just doing my duty for my children, what I feel fits." Many of those same people would return to me for help because they didn't have money for food. I would go to the warehouse and buy in bulk. I used to share. I did quite a lot of that; it's what my parents did at home in Jamaica, they taught me to do it, so I did.

Our search for accommodation went on for a year. We moved around black immigrant landlords to find suitable accommodation in six different addresses and it was very challenging.

The first home we bought was 14 St Peter's Road. We lived between two Irish families and they were quite good. They were very understanding and helpful towards my children and husband, as well as myself. Houses were not very expensive to purchase in 1957. My husband worked on the buses. I used to work in mental health and also ran a "partner savings finance club," so it was not a problem. It wasn't tricky to buy a house; you didn't have to have a large deposit and you didn't have to pay a high mortgage. When we bought the house on St Peter's Road, we paid £1,000 down then between £25-£26 per month. Some would be cheaper than that, depending on the size of the house.

Downstairs we had the front room, backroom, dining room, kitchen, and we had the toilet and bathroom at the back. On the first floor we had two rooms and, in the attic, there were two rooms. My husband's nephew had one and we lived in the big room upstairs. My first son had the other room in the attic because I never slept in the same room with my kids, they all had their own room, which was a privilege in the 1960s.

This is where my management and planning skills took centre stage. Whilst moving around, I got my first job, This was after three months at home doing hand-sewing and crocheting, needlework and planning a marriage. All with the prospect of difficult times ahead with racism, prejudice and discrimination within the white population. It was heart-breaking. There were racist remarks in shopping areas and even in churches, where peace and security in God's presence should be graceful. There was no place to hide. It was an unhappy time. Trapped in a world of uncertainty, life for many blacks and whites was impossible. It was the fittest of the strongest that survived the discrimination of those years. Those times were harrowing indeed. After the initial shock of the struggles, life's journey had to be faced courageously.

HAVING CHILDREN

Expecting a baby and working was very hard in February 1958. I endured a miscarriage in Dudley Road Hospital after an illness at work. In March, the process started all over again, I was pregnant. Arrangements for maternity leave were made in November 1958. When Arthur, my first baby was born, after the birth I had no one to assist me in caring for my child, so my only option was to stay at home, as home is where the family life is respected.

In 1960, my second child Collin was born then, in 1961, my third child, Bernadette. This is where my employment and working life ended, and the housewife domestic life situation began. What a journey. This is where God Almighty takes care of us all through prayers and providing for us within the family life unit. Working cheerfully makes for a rewarding, eventful occasion for everyone.

In 1966, Lilith, my fourth child, was born. Problems with milk digestion had occurred with Bernadette, and she was hospitalised for several years. A special diet had to be arranged for her under the care of Doctor Oldham. Her health improved and she was married at 19 years of age. She now has a teenaged daughter. Unfortunately, Bernadette was diagnosed with breast cancer in 2007. A breast was removed through the operation in a South Wales hospital, near where she lives. The operation was very difficult and caused a great deal of concern.

My fourth child, Lilith, lives and works in London with her two daughters, aged 13 and three years old. There is a constant worry when illness such as cancer and other killer diseases happen, because it affects family life. It is a very stressful situation. This is where faith in God plays an essential part in the recovery.

WORK

My first opportunity to work arose to explore work in the area of Aston in a cutlery factory and later in Hockley in a material sorting factory. The latter was very cold and therefore unsuitable for me to work in, so the experience only lasted two weeks. Both these jobs helped me to become familiar with the working conditions and government policy in Handsworth and the surrounding area of Birmingham.

After that experience, through the local newspaper I made an application to Highcroft Mental Health Hospital in Erdington, for the position of nursing/care assistant. My application was successful after my references were presented from Jamaican professionals. The resilience my mother had taught me was my lifeline in this particular plan of action, and this made working in a new country more manageable. In England, black immigrants were rarely considered to be as intelligent as the white inhabitants. Yet through my working life I met equal numbers of white individuals who had numeracy and literacy problems. The managers froze in astonishment when they saw the impressive references I had from educated individuals, despite being a poor young black lady from Jamaica who had travelled to England.

I worked three shifts, morning 7.30 a.m.-2 p.m., day shift 2 p.m.-6.30 p.m., night shift 8 p.m.-7.30 a.m. The wages in 1957 were £12-£15 per week, working four days on this three-shift system. The wards were managed by a matron and ward sister. There were at least two staff on at any one time. There were other staff members such as cleaners and dinner servers. If these were not in place, other staff would have to carry out the duties. The nursing and care assistant duties were to care for patients' needs on the wards, including changing bed linen, clothes, feeding, personal hygiene and communication skills. Watchful eyes and alertness were needed at all times because of the nature of the patients' illnesses. Individuals with mental health issues can be very unpredictable and have mood swings.

As black immigrants in workplaces, we all had another force to reckon with: racism. At its worst, the names that we were called showed undesirable discrimination at its core. I received this from patients and work colleagues.

I was earning much more money than my husband because I was in the NHS. I used to do long shifts. Sometimes four or five nights on with two nights off, and the people were awful; they were disrespectful, but I remained strong and respectable.

I said to one white lady, "you have the same blood in your body as I have, why do you hate me so much?" Then my boss came, and I told her the issue. I said, "you asked me to wash her, but she doesn't want me to, so I asked her the question and she won't answer." From then on things became quiet. They saw that I was doing the work right, but they used to complain about the other nurses, who were slapdash. If you need a wash or bath, then you're getting it from me whether you like it or not, because I'm paid to do a job. But I didn't shout or brawl like the rest, I was just quiet me. They were quite surprised at the manner in which I behaved, because I was taught from home how to behave. So, they were quite surprised. They didn't think that Jamaicans had education, manners or respect.

Training for qualified nursing status was offered but was very seldom taken up because of the abusive treatment black immigrants received in 1957, and still receive. Will this racial abusive ever cease? To pretend that racism no longer exists would be inaccurate.

I worked at the hospital from May 1957 until November 1958, when I left to give birth to my first child. I could have returned to work, but I had to no one to look after my son, so I stayed at home at those times at home, I was very lonely and missed my family. I began working from home with my children from November 1958 to 1970, there were complexities, difficulties, indifferences, hard work and struggles which had to be faced with responsibility, tolerance, honesty and justice.

As a responsible parent, the decision to stay at home looking after my children was an ethical one for me. My mother before me had done precisely the same and the rewards outweighed all the negative perceptions. I ran a dressmaking and alterations service, I placed a card advertising the service in the window of the house at St Peters Road, but local residents reported the card to Birmingham City Planning and Housing Department, I was visited by their representatives who explained the rules and regulations for Business and Private residential living areas. When we moved to Herbert Road in Handsworth we followed all of the procedures and the business thrived.

Working at home whilst caring for my children was an experience to cherish for the rest of my life. To my children and their friends, I was known as the no-nonsense parent. My communication was very straightforward, I didn't muddle my words. As a parent and a Christian, the rules and values of the house are very different. We all have to work together in every aspect for a sustainable and consistent outcome.

Most importantly, I was able to participate in my children's educational learning activities, and accomplished this with pride and dignity whilst being involved in the local community, volunteering and assisting others. Differences between black immigrants and white inhabitants were dissolved, when people realised that skin colour makes very little difference to respect, communication skills, tolerance, grace and humanity. The alternative would cause horrendous injustice and disastrous consequences.

Nevertheless, it is within these struggles that the whole family was able to survive through their educational pursuits. As a mother with four children, I studied English language, cookery and flower arranging at night school. It was imperative to learn these skills to make sure my children were well looked after and adjusted to the British way of life.

In order to have some stability and financial responsibility for my children and to pay the household bills, in 1963 I started a haberdashery and dressmaking business from home, and did this for approximately seven years. It was hard work, but it was worth every minute. It gave me a sense of responsibility towards my family. In addition to dressmaking, I also did a lot of alterations e.g. shortening dresses, adjusting shirt collars and cuffs, zips, button replacements, relining coats and jackets, making wedding dresses and other outfits. This was certainly one way of becoming involved in the local community, and it helped build stronger community cohesion and diversity. It certainly worked for me. Unfortunately, in 1970, all this ended because of a family crisis.

The English language is taught in schools and colleges in Jamaica, so communication was not a problem for me to converse with my children.

It is my belief that it is the duty of all parents to care for their children and make whatever sacrifices that have to be made in a positive and constructive manner for the benefit of the whole family. Unforeseen circumstances often mean it's necessary to try harder, and with help, life's journey can be made possible.

This educational journey has been accomplished by my family and myself. It was not easy but, by God's grace, we have achieved successful outcomes in education and jobs. My children are grown up and adore their mother. They also pass on what they were taught to their children. This has given them the stability to be prepared with dignity and pride for their higher educational journeys in universities.

Whilst at home, I developed community networking action, with careful planning and the involvement of local schools, parent and teacher associations, community associations, churches and wider local community group involvement. The respect of my own children's involvement was the highlight..

Most importantly the schemes had a profound and remarkable impact on their lives. Everyone has benefited from my mother's and grandmother's excellent parenting skills, which have been passed to others and been a defining moment of transition and integration towards tolerance and humanitarian efforts.

As a volunteer working in the local community, it has not always been comfortable, but positive thinking has helped to override severe conditions and concerns. It is the little things that make a difference and have been portrayed in community programmes. The way I have lived my life has manifested into excellent outcomes for future generations.

In spite of all the struggles, horrendous weather conditions, the most unwelcoming reception from a small group of English inhabitants, especially at a grassroots level, there have been dramatic changes in the integration process for black immigrants. The English educational process of learning and harsh working conditions in parts has been very educational and wonderfully served. This would have not been so very acceptable to me without my family's training in my early years.

My grandmother had a tremendous human conscience and kindness for the poor, she took a respectable approach for the benefit of others. She worked tirelessly to serve the local community during the twentieth century. She began to show signs of ill health at the age of 95. Her daughter nursed her until her death at 97 years old. In her nursing career, she cared for the local community and built bridges consistently whilst supplying specialist care towards the needs of new-born babies, often in harmful and devastating conditions. She showed determination, hard work, obedience and an excellent attitude towards life in spite of the difficulties.

I was in Handsworth, England, when she died, with my own sewing business My mother asked me to make a dress for her to be buried in, so I did. There is a photograph of the dress in the Birmingham museum. I made the dress and thought, "well, I'm not sending it her until I try it on myself", because my measurements were 36, 36, 36, the same as my grandmother. I was quite slim until I had the kids, but I've changed now.

I sent it to her and it cost me about £12 to box it up, because I did a white veil and hat. I waited for the answer and mom said she was still alive. Then she said the reason why she had sent for it was that she wanted to be prepared for her funeral. It was 12 years later that she died, and she wore that dress. It was the 1980s when she died. I was unable to visit Jamaica for my grandmother's funeral service because of my children. I was emotionally upset due to not being able to attend, but there was nothing I could do.

In the 1950s, racism was the norm. When black immigrants moved into a house in any street, whites moved on even if neighbours wanted to stay with their friends. There were very little tolerance and a large amount of hate. It was the same when black immigrants wanted to purchase goods from shops. When any purchase was made, the shopkeeper made sure he didn't touch the buyer when receiving the money; any change was always placed on the counter for the black immigrants to take.

There were also signs on shops and other places that said, No blacks, No Irish, No dogs.

That happened a lot too after the riots started in 1985. Then, the young people started rebelling because they had no place to live or work. Initially they said it was the blacks that were causing the riots, but police investigations later said it was the white youths that started it because they didn't want to see us living here. They were terrible times. I went into a shop and the man asked me if he could see my passport. I didn't reply, just smiled.

In spite of all these struggles, it was my childhood upbringing that assisted me with the confidence to work hard in sight of humiliation received, with God's grace and mercy, and to take a positive approach to hard work at home and at work, to make a difference to others. I like to do the work and take pleasure in doing it and look at the finished product, knowing that I did it well. I do all the painting and decorating. I do everything. I never moan. I know what and how I want. I wanted a set life structure for my children. All of my friends used to come and visit they would say, oh dear, you are working hard, but I'm not waiting on my husband to do work in the home, I'm living in it all day long.

There is no use arguing with my husband and waiting for him to do it. I know what I want, so I just got on with it.

I also told my grandma the facts as I observed them, you know, what happened, how people behaved etc. In letters, I said to grandma: "it's a good job I knew about racism before I came to England here." Because of my background through my grandmother's marriage, I knew about racism because of the white and black situation within my family. There were also other families in the very same position as we were. I also found out when I came here that, of many of the people I lived with, I was the only person who could read and write. There were limited educational learning skills for hundreds of both black and white families.

I was asked to write letters for individuals when they found out that I was able to read and write. There was a large number who were not able to communicate with their families in Jamaica because of their lack of education. I was pleased and willing to assist those who needed help. Sometimes, if they asked other people to write and send their money home for them, their relatives would not get the money because the supposed writer would keep the money or send it to their own family. So I would write, and the people would receive their money and letters. Being honest in life is the best way to be.

It was here in England that highlighted the understanding of slavery and racism a lot of West Indian individuals had endured through the landowner workforces in Jamaica. Some had no educational training whatsoever to assist them in their lives.

Here I am wearing the dress I made for my grandmother's funeral
A letter from my Mother

Chapter Eight

Marriage & Divorce

"I BELIEVE I DEALT VERY HONESTLY AND FAIRLY WITH MY HUSBAND IN EVERY MANNER. OF COURSE, THIS EXTRAORDINARY JOURNEY HAD REACHED ITS CLIMAX."

I arrived in February and got married in September 1957. The wedding took place on 21st of September 1957 at the Registrar Office in Broad Street, Edgbaston. The reception was held at one of the rooms in our let home, 113 Wellington Road, Handsworth, Birmingham. There was no access to renting public buildings for social activities or weddings for black immigrants. The wedding was beautiful, and we had approximately 50 guests. After the wedding, another move was arranged because of uncomfortable living in communal homes.

In November 1958, my first child was born and within eight years, we had four children. Unfortunately, the love dangerously diminished between Chandla and I, the situation was horrendous.

In 1971, a divorce was unavoidable. I was perplexed and dispirited for many years after the divorce, but life had to go on. I felt a more powerful Christian focus and life became less stressful and more inspirational. This is where the hard work really began within my divine Christian purpose, and also looking after my children. I thank God for every day.

Yesterday's, today's and future generations who decide to marry and live together as a couple will have some difficulties. These difficulties can be solved if attention is given to the issues as they arise. The couple, both the husband and wife must prioritise and deal with marital difficulties. The way that we have been raised influences how we deal with challenges that arise in adulthood.

My husband came from a very wealthy family, he did not receive parental training, as he was nursed and raised by nannies in his early years. My husband's father was a white plantation owner and his mother half-caste. his mother wanted him to marry me, because she thought he was coming into a family with principles and discipline. Chandla had a high standard of education but was very lazy in home life maybe because of his privileged childhood upbringing. I felt that once we had children, he grew uncomfortable and restless. I could not understand why, because he wanted children, but he could just not cope with life's responsibilities.

My expectations of marriage and my husband were shattered when I discovered diary entries that revealed that my husband had been unfaithful and I now had to seriously put my strength and energies into my children's welfare and well-being. I cried and prayed. There was no domestic violence involved, but there was the destruction of household contents, for example, the wedding album.

I used to write letters to my mother and explain what was happening and she would reply to me and reminded me about keeping family business private and how to manage my Christian faith. Prayer kept me steadfast and strong. Sometimes I go out walking and think about it. I just take my time and do what I have to do, and God takes control. My God has never, never let me down., Honestly, I cannot think of a time when I call on the Lord , or kneel down to pray, that I don't feel his presence. I'm so grateful for God guiding me through all of this and making sure I understand about His saving grace through reading scriptures for comfort. These were always a blessing for me.

I had to use wisdom as a way of protection for myself and my family, and I knew that was my responsibility. I am aware that when I agreed to marry Chandla, I didn't fully take on board some of the advice given to me by his mother, I didn't take it all in as I was excited about the opportunity to travel to England.

After the horrendous situation, I tried to be tolerant, respectful, honest and hard-working through the hard times, including the divorce proceedings. I divorced my husband. He did not divorce me. As part of the divorce proceedings, I specifically asked to remain in the home with the children so that their education wasn't disrupted and there was no change to their short journey to school, which was within walking distance. This was granted and, because of this, I did not seek any other financial rewards, after maintenance, for the children and myself.

After several years, my ex-husband journeyed to Jamaica and approached my mother to ask if I would reconsider and remarry him. The answer was most definitely no. He then demanded a cash settlement from the house from me; this was arranged through the solicitors who managed the divorce proceedings.

He went off to America, married again and died of a brain tumour. In the days of his illness, he telephoned me almost every day. Collin, our son, visited him through his illness and returned with his brother Arthur and sister Bernadette when he died in 1990 in America. Here one life journey ends and his children continue the life-long process of living.

Nothing ever works out how individuals want it to be. It was and is the inner strength gained through the Christian lifestyle and prayerful intercession which helps us cope in times of distress, and especially during the breakdown of a marriage and divorce, which is and was horrendous. That said, there are successful achievements in marriages that have inspired many others. My mother and stepfather's marriage was one of these.

I am so pleased that my parents taught me how understanding others and myself is crucial, and this is how I relate to other individuals needing help. Many times, people have come to talk to me about their marriage difficulties. They didn't know about my troubles, but through telling me about there's, they recounted similar troubles to ones I've experienced.

With marital issues, I direct them to a solicitor. I would say the best thing to do is go to a solicitor because I cannot interfere in other people's business. Some of the wives used to come to me for sewing, but sometimes their husbands would come to check and they weren't there. The wife had gone somewhere else and told their husband they were with me. I'm not a talker, so I didn't speak, so when the husbands came, I would say, "you can look, but they are not here." Black and white women are all similar. I wouldn't talk. and when the ladies came to me the next time, some of them would say something, and some wouldn't. I'd say, "your husband came to find you, but you were not here." Their face would turn red and I knew, but I didn't say anything or ask them questions.

I would listen to other women about the violence they experienced from their husbands, I didn't have that problem with my husband, but we had to divorce.

I divorced my husband on the basis of his unreasonable behaviour, through the courts, and he was found guilty by his very own hand-written confessions. My husband told me during the divorce proceedings that the way he lived was his way of life, and he would not change for anyone, and so it was.

My love for my husband remains because it was so hard to separate the love of my children from the love of my husband, but in life's journey, individuals have to make sacrifices in complex situations and also make appropriate decisions and changes for the future, this, I did.

To be a woman and divorced is always bad news for onlookers because they haven't heard or witnessed some of the causes that make the situation unbearable for both concerned.

Life has to go on and after 15 years of marriage, we were divorced. I was left to parent four children single-handedly for the rest of my life. Divorce creates severe, stressful health problems for both adults and their children. But through my life, I have been able to cope with life's difficulties reasonably well and in good health. I would say to any individual to be prayerful and hard-working; be honest and God will be listening to your cry and will help you with your struggles. I was personally helped in many different ways.

When two people get married, for most of us our thoughts are never on separation, but some consideration should be given on the topic of divorce because it is also possible. Divorce can be distressing. Every nerve in our human body is dismantled, stress takes over, and difficulties emerge. Everyone involved is devastated by what has happened, but the desire is to continue to do our best for all who are involved, especially the children. My Christian faith kept me focused on my survival skills. Hard work pays dividends, and I thank God for the loving care received.

After being at home as a responsible parent for my four young children, it was time to get work, which would satisfy our financial needs.

In 1977 I applied for a night care nursing assistant position, to care for senior citizens. This would enable me to both be employed and maintain the same high standard of care for my four children/teenagers. The application was successful. In one of the interviews, I was asked, "if you are at work and one of your children was caught by the police on Soho Road, how would you deal with the incident?"

My answer was, "it would never happen." and it didn't happen, thank God. All my children were prepared to assist their mother to earn money to help them. Working together with the great understanding needed to be a principal aim and objective. They understood even when life's expectancies and struggle came very early for my children, and they seemed to manage very well indeed.

The duties for night shifts in 1977 were from 10 p.m.-7:30 a.m. at Camden Street, Hockley, Birmingham. The work duties were caring for the elderly. Sometimes they were very ill patients for whom death was inevitable. The care had to be very patient-focused and intense and was accompanied by writing detailed reports and other documentation. I did enjoy the work very much, although of course, when someone dies, we were overshadowed by sadness for their families left behind, the work experience I gained was invaluable. As soon as a more flexible, daytime shift became available, I changed over, so I could be at home at night with my children. This was in 1978.

I then applied to the Social Services Children's Department for a job as a cook for children in care. This was very rewarding indeed, and I was in the catering profession for years. The opportunity for me to study at Sutton Coldfield College to enhance my catering skills one day a week was very encouraging, and I did this for three years. Through the college, I learnt about preparation, decoration and presentation of all types of food. I even restarted my catering business professionally. In 1985 after approximately 10 years working in Social Services, I decided to open a Fish & Chip Shop with a Caribbean Take Away, I ran this for two years, with my children's assistance in the evenings. What an experience that was! My children were delighted for me, as well as for themselves; I worked in my job part-time and ran the business for the rest of the time. After a while, we all became tired , it was heavy going running a business and working and for the children, it was a great deal of pressure. After two years of operating, we decided to close the business.

My husband and I with our first child in the 1960's

Chapter Nine

Raising My Children Alone

There are very few families who could ever say that it's not difficult to raise children into respectful adults. In my home discipline, respect, church life and educational opportunities with learning experiences were part of life from an early age. Time limits were set for working at home so that they would be comfortable at school. Whatever they were all learning at home helped them in their schoolwork and also in being responsible citizens in the local wider community.

Parents have to teach children the right way to develop and accept the rules and boundaries set. Parents also have a responsibility to see that they carry out their own duties to their children daily. One of the best responsibilities I have ever fulfilled in my life's journey was to be at home with my children for 19 years, to make sure that they worked hard on their education, their literacy and numeracy and all other subjects studied, just as I had when I was back home with my family in Jamaica.

Please do not believe that I do not value the challenges and struggles or that I am in any way suggesting that children are not difficult to manage, but as parents, we have to be focused and stay steadfast and reliable to achieve our goals together.

My children would say that I am a strict mother; I raised them with discipline, and they had to keep to my rules, or there were consequences.

One evening, my sons were supposed to be having a little play outside and were due to come back in at 6 p.m. They went off with their friends to the park and didn't come back until about 9-9:30 p.m. I was upstairs in the home and they were knocking the front door, I could hear them talking, they didn't have a key. I didn't give my children a key the rule was if they didn't come back on time , and If I wasn't in, they would have had to wait until I had come back. They wanted to come in, but I would not let them in, I said, "unless you go up to the police station and bring the police down here with you, you will not be sleeping in my house tonight," as simple as that.

The next thing I knew, a policeman knocked on the door, I opened the door to him and could see my boys behind him; he said, "I have two lads here, I presume they are yours?"

I replied, "I presume they are mine, aren't they?"

"What have they been doing?" He asked.

I said, "didn't they tell you?"

So, they had to stand there and explain to the policeman that they had come home late and were not allowed in. The policeman asked to come in and wanted to know where the boys would be sleeping. I asked, "what do you want to know that for then?" "you can take them upstairs and let them see where you sleep."

When he came back down, he said, "lads, the two of you have a room and bed each, you're not sleeping together." He was amazed about that, actually, because in those days many children slept in one bed together. So, he said, "well, you hear what your mother says, I'm telling you now, that my children don't have their own bedroom, don't let me ever hear about you two again." It never happened again.

I was strict with my children for many reasons. I'm looking after my children because I'm giving them the best attention, and the best they can have. I'm their mother, and it is my responsibility to look after them well, to get the best results. I never complained about being a single parent; I just did the job as I had to do the job, with pride and honesty.

When my children had birthdays, they would invite their teachers, and they would be delighted to visit and say, "this house is well polished." We used to do barbecues out the back with the other children. You see, that's the way I was brought up. My grandmother used to invite all the kids and do these sorts of educational activities for them, so I wasn't afraid of doing it here in England. Then teachers and other adults would know that I don't mess around. I was serious about education and proper upbringing.

When my children were at primary school, and I went for a parent-teacher meeting, I saw work displayed in which the spellings were wrong. When I went up, I said, "why is my child's work on the wall?"

The teacher said, "well, it is excellent work."

"But," I said, "the spelling is wrong."

So, he said, "well, we allow that."

I said, "well, as long I'm standing here, I won't be moving until it's moved from the wall, because the spelling is wrong."

When we got home, I ensured that they did the spellings enough times to get it right.

The teachers had low expectations and low standards for the kids. Children will not learn that way, and I wasn't having that. They are expecting them to be under-achievers. My hope was that my children would learn, be educated more than I am and later earn much more money than me too. My role as a mother was to ensure that my children had a good education and qualifications. I bought books on how to teach my children and I was a school governor, I was not accepting low expectations of mine or other peoples children.

In the 1970's both of my sons were to attend grammar school, yet they at first would only accept one of them. A lot of parents couldn't challenge that decision, but I could. I went to the school and I said, "Shall I call the newspaper?"

They responded, "we didn't know that you knew anything about the newspapers!" This was blatant racism at its core.

Of course, it may have been easier if their father had been around as well, but only if both of us were singing from the same hymn sheet. I was pining for my husband because I didn't really want to part from him, but I just got on with it and looked after the children, because that was my responsibility.

To those who are embarking on marriage, or having children I advise that you support your children, teach them the right way to live, teach them how to respect themselves and others because, if they don't respect themselves, if they have a wife and children, they are not going to get that respect. They have to have respect for themselves to hand it out to their children. I made sure of that with mine. If a woman has lost their partner, is divorced or separated, they should do what I did. When I was alone I prayed and I cried. I talked to the Lord himself, and said, "you are the one that gives me knowledge, strength and understanding. These children are my responsibility, you know why I am alone with them."

Then I just got on with it. If they were spoilt, it would be the mother's fault. If the children are horrible, it's mother that was looking after them. I would get the hard knock of it because I didn't do it right. I So, I had to make sure they understood. When we have family dinners now, they sit and they say, "oh mommy, well we can always say that you did it right for us." Then I roll my eyes and ask, "are you talking to me?"

I never let my children sleep away from home, only on school trips, no sleeping out. They come to their home at night, no sleeping out. When they go to other homes and they have different rules, they would get confused; they would want to take the rules into my home, and I wouldn't want that, it was as simple as that. You must think about what you want for your children. How do you think people are going to talk about you and your family? Lots of people knew I had children. They have never gone into friends' homes. They would say, "mommy, can my friends come along? I would say, "when you're talking about your friends coming, they must first ask their parents.

Overall, my children tell me I was tough, so I got that one wrong. They said I was too tough, but I told them not to worry about it, you're here now. I don't get angry, I had to make the rules, I was bringing the food in, I had to do everything.

I would just move away, kneel down and pray, and do what I have to. I know in my heart that I'm doing the right thing, I never changed. If I put the rules down, the rules remain. There was one instance, when I talked to one of my children and he got huffy; He stormed out and slammed the door. I said, "remember what I say. If you want to get any pocket money for the next three months, don't ask me, because you're not getting a penny. If the door comes off the hinges, you'll be paying for new hinges and someone to put them on. So, when you're ready to close the door properly, please do." I meant every word that I said I would not do anything differently if I had to be in charge of my children again in 2019.

My eldest son was in music, and he has Grade 8 qualifications in playing the flute and other musical instruments in the school orchestra. He did stage management for musicians as his first job in London. I didn't allow him to become a musician for a profession as I didn't want him to get mixed up in the music lifestyle of drugs and sex, My responsibility was to protect him, so he pursued an alternative career. I am pleased that later in life he did take up music again, however.

My daughters also think I was extremely strict, because the first daughter, when she was getting married, wanted to sleep over at her husband's home. I don't know why she bothered to ask, because she knew I would say no. But they did try. I could assess all the friends that came in. I said friends could come in, but they are not allowed upstairs. They stay downstairs until they are ready to go. They are not running around, all over my house. They think I wasn't relaxed. I explained to my children that I did not wish to see anything go wrong, exactly how my parents would say it to me.

Once a month, I would do something special like Curry Pattie, or a Jamaican dish, and they'd sit in the living room, with a tray. We usually eat at the dining table. I would say, "this is the time you can talk about me, tell me what you think about me." They would say, "even if we told you, you wouldn't take any notice." I would say, "well, I would love to hear anyway." Now that they are older, they appreciate that they had an excellent, steady upbringing.

They are all respectable, and in good jobs, I am proud of them. My Eldest son holds a BSc and MSc degree, My young son is a quantity surveyor at the highest level; he has done well for himself. Despite her health challenges my eldest daughter has always worked in catering and retail. My youngest daughter worked at Buckingham Palace for about 19 years, with The Not Forgotten organisation, until she had her second daughter. She is living in London. Sometimes I would travel down to London to help with the children. She now works with another company and Transport for London.

All of my children are very hard-working, and so too are all of my grandchildren. Marcus was in the Royal Air Force for seven to eight years. My children have all bought property, and they don't waste their finance. When they were children almost every Saturday morning, if I gave them a few pence in pocket money, half of it had to go in the bank. So, Saturday morning, every one of them would go to the bank, and every one of them left my home with a bank account, with money in it.

At Christmas time they take me out. Last time the little one took me out and wanted to buy me a pair of boots for £150. I said, "no, I'm not having it. I'll have a pair of boots but you're not spending £150 on me."

When they were growing up and I'm cooking, they all had to come in the kitchen. They all have to learn, so they can do their own cooking. I said to the sons, "look, if you have a wife and children, and you and the wife fall out, how are you going to eat? You can't be spending money out there buying food when you can do it yourself." So, all of them learnt the basic skills. I've never gone to any of their homes and found them dirty. Everything is always in place, because that it is the way they are.

Life was difficult at times,especially financially, but our bills had to be paid, I worked hard, I was sensible with money and I paid my bills. It would have been wrong to create bad debts. Children need stability to be able to function and to thrive; my children participated in the Boys Brigade, Brownies and Girl Guides, I ensured that they were involved in the local community.

They suffered racism being black children of immigrants, because of my awareness of this I felt it was my duty to be on the school governors board and to make my presence felt within the school and educational environment. I have four children two boys and two girls, nine grandchildren and one great-grandchild. Five of my grandchildren are in or have completed higher education degrees, Marcus, my grandson, followed his grandfather and served in the Royal AirForce. My offspring have excelled in behaviour towards everyone whom they came into contact with over the years.

My First Husband Chandla McGhie working as a Bus Conductor

Chapter Ten

Married Life with Reginald Belgrave

After twenty years of being divorced, I got married for the second time to an 81-year-old Christian senior, Mr Reginald Belgrave. My second husband came from Barbados in the 1950s. He worked in the building trade as a crane driver.

He was a true believer in Christianity. It was his Christian lifestyle that attracted the love of us both to each other. Mr Belgrave had been married, but his wife had died several years prior.

My second marriage gained me a more direct inner focus on scripture and spiritual acknowledgement of how to develop my life's expectations in Christianity because, together, we were both working towards the same goals for a wonderful life. The few years we spent together, we achieved a few of our goals.

Mr Reginald Belgrave lived in Stechford village in Birmingham. I moved there in January 1992. We had a formal wedding ceremony on May 6th, 1995. It took six months of planning and lots of preparation with my husband's friends and family and also my friends and family. We created a most beautiful and memorable day of my life.

This was a church wedding with 350 guests at Aston Christian Centre in Thomas Street, Aston, Birmingham, conducted by Reverend Calvin Young. The wedding service was a wonderful occasion. The wedding presentations and catering were carried out by myself, my sister, my niece, and close friends. All my children and grandchildren played an important part in the whole of the presentations, ceremonies, and reception. It was a glorious and wonderfully blessed event. All my family had taken part responsibly.

The most interesting and memorable impact of the day's events were the host community's respectful contribution and participation in the wedding service and reception. The yellow Rolls-Royce was magnificent. Photographs were taken in Handsworth Park and The Church Hall and the reception was also held in Handsworth.

My husband had been a Christian for 61 years and played an active part in several churches. He also was a member of a church choir. He was a member at Aston Christian Centre, at Thomas Street, Aston. He was a very mature and musical. What I enjoyed most was we both could enjoy reading the Bible scripture with great understanding. He told me once he would have liked to have been a police officer.

My husband had been ill for a considerable time with his heart and cancer problems. With hard work and loving care, we had four years of married life together. In 1997, through his illness, I had to retired from my work, which I clearly loved, to care for him before he died in July 1999.

To be a carer for my husband was both difficult and hard work. It was at times distressing to have to watch him being in pain, disorientated and taking high doses of medication for his cancer. His funeral service was as lovely as our wedding ceremony. The weather conditions were delightful, although the day was very emotional.

He had finished the end of life's journey, restoring in peace in the grave where he lies. To be alone is not extremely easy to comprehend, yet everyone will face death sooner or later in their lives.

Mourning for my husband after his death as a Christian was very difficult. It's the loneliness which had the greatest impact on my life. My local friends, my family and my community involvement has assisted in my healing process. Thank God I had made the right choice.

My marriage to my second husband, Mr Reginald Belgrave, is somehow like the Bible reading in Matthew 8 v23-27, which speaks of the great tempest in the sea where the ship was covered with waves and Jesus' disciples were fearful and woke him. After asking about their fearfulness, Jesus rebuked the winds, and the sea became calm. Also Psalm 23 v4:- even though I walk through the valley of the shadow of death I will fear no evil for you are with me your rod and your staff they comfort me.

There are many rough passages, and there were many smooth paths, but with much determination, I have struggled for survival and now I am enjoying the benefit of my hard work. It is also through my integrity and the principles of my spiritual faith and a stable childhood that all these factors have sustained me to capture several memorable magical moments in historical period settings.

The day I left work to retire and care for my husband

Stechford Baptist is a small community church in East Birmingham, near Stechford Station. About thirty children and fifteen young people regularly take part in Sunday activities.

It was founded at the beginning of the twentieth century, and the church bought land for a large building in the 1920s. In the way of things, because of the Great Depression, only a temporary building could be built which occupied a small part of the land. seventy-seven years later, the temporary building is still standing – and all but a small corner of the land was sold off for housing in the 1970s.

The small corner of land that was left was grassed over, but was largely rubble from the housing projects.

In 2003 Mrs Eunice McGhie-Belgrave and Mr David Lawton led the church into a garden project, to turn the small corner of land into a garden, growing vegetables as a way of helping children and young people to learn about God's goodness. By 2005, the garden was producing enough to fill a huge harvest table at the harvest festival, which made Stechford Baptist look more like a countryside church than an urban one.

The project was recently given an award by Birmingham City Council. Mrs McGhie-Belgrave and Mr Lawton are now working with other church members to extend the project and give it more impact in the community. B-CEN has begun to express interest in it. Mrs McGhie-Belgrave was one of the leaders of the Uplands Allotment Project.

Too see more please visit the Shades of Black website and send your comments to our email address.

Website: www.sobhelpproject.org.uk
Email: sobhelpproject@yahoo.co.uk

Chapter Eleven

Cancer My Hands-on Experience

My first husband had a brain tumour and the subsequent operation was not successful. Although I had minimal contact with him after our divorce, it was nevertheless heart-breaking.

With my second husband, I was his carer, when he was ill with cancer of the colon. It was stressful to work in such close proximity to someone so ill and it created many anxious moments. The high dosage of medication prescribed caused disruption to his whole-body functions and daily routines had suddenly changed. His quality of life disintegrated, with sudden death taking precedence over life in a flash.

As my husband's carer, a decision had to be made; do I stay in the job that I have loved so much, or retire to be with him at home as my bound duty demanded? Staying at home was very difficult but, as I am used to hard work, it was a pleasure to fulfil such intricate and personal duties for others. This is where prayers from Christian friends and inner strength pays dividends, and God knows it all.

I was also involved in community action and had managed a successful community project presenting hands-on basic skills with local school pupils through the allotment project. A plan of action was put into place to combat disappointment. With the help of John Taylor Hospice respite care and the assistance of volunteers, my community work continued. There were several distressing moments. It is tough to be a personal carer for anyone with cancer. Care has to be personal, hands-on, and managed well, which involves hard work. He had two years of excellent home care. Here my duties were accomplished. These years were challenging. He became disruptive, restless and experienced weight loss, and it was distressing to watch him suffer endlessly in pain.

Through my Christian lifestyle, I was prepared for his death. He took ill on the Monday and was admitted to hospital on the Tuesday. He died on the Thursday in July 1999. Whilst in the moment it was heartbreaking, it was also a blessing at the same time. Because everything was already planned, life became easier to manage. After the funeral service, it was the loneliness at night that was draining and depressing at times, but reading the scriptures with great understanding and praying to the 'Lord God in heaven' has assisted in my struggles of acceptance, which have provided the inner strength that is needed in living.

I have always had the capability and capacity for hard work, so I went back to work for a further four years in the education service in schools, with primary and secondary pupils, within basic life skills programmes, whilst still working on the community projects within Handsworth and Stechford in Birmingham.

Just when I thought everything was going fine, one of my daughters was diagnosed with breast cancer in 2004, and my son with cancer of the bladder in 2009. After the instant anxiety and shock waves through my system, the hard work of acceptance began. Continued lifetime support began. It is never easy when it's your very own children that are ill, especially when it's cancer. I was encouraged by the first-hand experience gained from my husband's illness because I learnt how to manage in these unforeseen circumstances. I thank God for his watchful eyes upon me as he gave me the inner strength to cope.

At the moment, life is extremely difficult for one of my children and more comfortable for the other. But I know that more uncomfortable days are yet to surface. When it comes, I am ready to embrace the challenges and consequences with joy and delight. Once again, our family circumstances have changed sadly, cancer returned to my daughter in 2018, and because of concerns about her, she is being monitored very closely at the moment. The journey of life's struggles has manifested itself.

The only advice I can personally give is to be very positive and forward-thinking. Focus on the very best that presents itself in any circumstance.

In terms of my own health, at the age of 79 years in 2014, I was diagnosed with a lack of Vitamin D2. There is no known cure and I also have arthritis in my shoulders. When the news was revealed, all I said was, "my time has come." Since I have been living in England, I have had no major illness. Age has undoubtedly not yet stopped my hard work in community action projects. These projects were moved to my home for me to continue to deliver them as I moved up in age.

I believe it was the right decision to move the project around to be home-based. It is more manageable and is fulfilling the needs of local people, who want to learn and integrate with others in Stechford, where I have lived since 1992. Now At 85 years of age, no medical conditions are preventing me from living my full life potential .

1957
I flew from Palisadoes Airport Kingston, Jamaica to London Airport England

Chapter Twelve

Reflection

I TRAVELLED TO ENGLAND, FROM THE BEAUTIFUL CARIBBEAN ISLAND OF JAMAICA

to be married to ex-soldier Chandla Davidson and live in Birmingham in the early 1950s.

As a black immigrant who had journeyed from the Caribbean to England, I was shocked on arrival by the harsh frosty weather conditions and the racism, which was at its peak then but still exists now. In the 22 years I lived in the Caribbean, I was always motivated by education, hard-working the inspirational guidance from my mother and grandmother.

I wondered if it would be possible to adjust to the very different weather conditions in England, and when I spoke to others from the Caribbean, they felt the same desperation. Many had sold their prized possessions to make the journey, seeking greater financial rewards and a more settled life. It was disappointing and very difficult to adjust to the living conditions.

I was facing a different reality. We had been led to believe England had very high and humane standards. As Jamaicans, we too were British subjects, until our independence in 1985.

During my education, I was taught and read many publications which implied the streets of England were paved with gold, but hundreds of people who had travelled before me had yet to witness the golden streets of England.

Another problem for black immigrants was language. In Jamaica, in elementary and secondary school, we were taught the English language but at grass roots level.

Patois was also spoken and the difficulties were that, in England, black immigrants were not easily understood verbally because their basic communications skills were misunderstood by their white counterparts

I was a poor, illegitimate child growing up in the West Indies, with struggles and challenges which became more apparent at times. I was brought up believing in education, hard work and serving our community. With this wisdom and understanding of life. I have embraced opportunities, I have achieved and accomplished much more than I could ever have conceptualised. Including being awarded numerous times for my lifelong contribution to society in the UK.

In the next part of this book you will read about and see examples of the projects I have initiated and implemented in my local community, I pray that you will be inspiured by my contribution.

Part Two
Introduction

COMMUNITY ACTION NETWORKING IN ENGLAND

Putting others first, is a respectable way of working together also, it is an excellent way of learning basic life skills which benefit us all. This will continue to be the ethos of my projects with the young, my own goals and objectives and also within Shades of Black research and programme of activities.

"Education Is Key"

Throughout the early years of life, the involvement with local community people participation in the beautiful island of Jamaica in the Parish of St James Maldon District rural countryside where natural activities sequences of programme events which was relevant to the catering needs of human well-being service delivery had always presented through churches, schools and the wider Local Communities.

To achieve high standards in life, it is true to say hard work is needed for consistency, excellent education, communication, good attitude, tolerance, humility, respect towards others, not being self-opinionated, gracefulness and humanity towards our fellow mankind. All these meaningful words must be seen to be portrayed in everyday working life to be a positive focus in the dreams we all desire to be fulfilled.

The training received through my grandmother, mother, family members, the local older generation and elementary school education had been my legacy, and a positive role model throughout my life. This is where my community action networking began.

My personal encounter in community action networking within local communities in Handsworth, Aston and Stechford since 1960-2019 in England, took place whilst parenting my family. I made myself available, and this is where my children's knowledge of catering for the needs of the most vulnerable young and senior citizens of all nationalities was learnt. It continued throughout my working life, helping in the simple tasks to make things better for others in the Handsworth area.

Shades of Black ~ Volunteering

THERE WERE UNPREDICTABLE CHALLENGES AND STRUGGLES. IT WAS A JOURNEY OF DEVELOPMENT AND SOCIAL INTEGRATION, WHILST CREATING A STRONGER COMMUNITY LINK **THROUGH SOCIAL DIVERSITY COHESION WITHIN THE WIDER COMMUNITY. RACISM WAS VERY, VERY RIFE. "NO IRISH. NO DOGS. NO BLACKS."**

I had not realised that the way of life chosen in England would result in an inspiring role model for thousands of individuals. Since the 1960s, when the idea of community action networking began, I had profound, life-changing influences and involvement within the local community. My children's education became an important issue of debatable subject where social life contacts were extremely and delicately, as redefined colour bar was very much a hindrance and concern within the local community lifestyle.

These periodic and problematic times were very difficult to manage, because it was common to blame black immigrants.

Nevertheless, it had to be fixed through black and white people working together and learning from each other to develop some kind of mutual understanding through basic educational skills learning.

During the early years of the project, funding was received from the Probation Aftercare Service, and SOB committee members did raffles every month at 36 Hebert Road, Handsworth, and programmes of activities presentation were 228 Hamstead Road Handsworth Birmingham Probation service. From 1989-1997, Shades of Black Committee members' programmes were very educational, for adults and children. Visits to farms, Ryton Organic Gardens and museums were included, and we made hats for Easter and Halloween. The children learnt new games and artwork, and parents loved the educational inspiration.

For adult and senior citizens, educational programmes through north Birmingham College were arranged e.g. first aid, health and safety and food hygiene.

In-house activities were flower arranging, sewing, cookery and educational awareness programmes e.g. aids awareness, mental health awareness and historical stories of Handsworth. Most of the programmes were on Saturdays, because all SOB members and volunteers work during the week. Also, we were able to give parents respite from their children. Easter bonnet programmes always have over 150 children in attendance, with at least 25 parents also present. They loved the radio interviews that were arranged.

Accessing funding for activities was always set as a debatable subject item in the monthly meetings. Funds were also accessed from the local police, as they were also involved in our activities from 1989-1997. Other organisations such as local churches and schools had participated in our project presentations.

In 1989, diversity induction cohesion programmes by Shades of Black were very much an acceptable norm. It was at an exhibition of Handsworth's history, displayed at Handsworth Boys' School, where I was approached to participate in the Uplands Allotment Project, hence the "Help" enables Learning Positively or positive learning enables help came into being.

As a school governor at the only girls' school, I approached Dr Nepausingh OBE, the head teacher, with a networking project idea. He was approachable and supportive of the project plan, funding application to Shell Better Britain Oil Company were submitted three times = £3,600. With eight girls of Handsworth Wood secondary girl's school in 1998, this was certainly the beginning of the unique "Help" Uplands Allotment Project.

To be involved in the development of such a wonderful, educational, pupils' healthy living lifestyle project, which has been a great interactive role model for young people with the assistance of the media, is a wonderful achievement.

Within the "Help" Uplands Allotment Project, pupils participated in a new way of learning basic life skills in an open-air classroom.

Voluntary work and Studying

I started this on my own in the 1960s as a black immigrant in England, to keep up my home tradition, as my parents had taught me through my Christianity and elementary education. I had discovered that I was able to improve my educational standard whilst at home caring for my children through evening classes once per week through two-hour sessions, and so I did. I then volunteered with West Midlands Probation Service.

I worked in the Probation Aftercare Service as a volunteer for 20 years. In May 1988, I was successful in my application to be a Cultural Cook Supervisor at Handsworth Cultural Centre. Within this role, I developed a programme entitled good housekeeping and independent living for the client base, and also offered basic education skills, teaching/learning opportunities for young offenders and 'let's talk' sessions, in line with the Probation Service's equal opportunities policy. The programme was very versatile, sensitive and efficiently equipped in a form that was tailor-made to meet the client's particular needs.

The programme has proved flexible, practical and easy to grasp, and has been used as part of an educational facility at various local prisons, such as Brinsford, as well as being part of a rolling programme at Handsworth Cultural Centre with both clients and students.

Through my in-depth hard work with the Probation Aftercare Service, my academic training at Birmingham Polytechnic/Birmingham University was financed by the Probation Service. I studied Community and Advice work and graduated in 1992.

This enhanced my ability to manage the clients' work with consistency and loving care. I was also promoted to the position of Assistant probation officer (APO). It was a proud moment at the age of 58 to wear my cap and gown and be awarded my qualification in the presence of my children.

Shades of Black Research

Mental Health Project for All Nationalities.

The programme was about research on how adequately developed mental health services could be accessed by black people compared to the white community. The findings were disturbing indeed. As a result we developed a mental health awareness project and worked with schools to devise a play called "Something Inside So Strong" presented to The Lord Mayor of Birmingham in Handworth Wood Girls School. We then as members of SOB were nominated for a Healthcare Award, we were awarded second place at an event at the Houses of Parliament, we were presented with a certificate and cash to continue our research on 23rd January 1997 The highlight of the visit was seeing so many MP's in attendance.

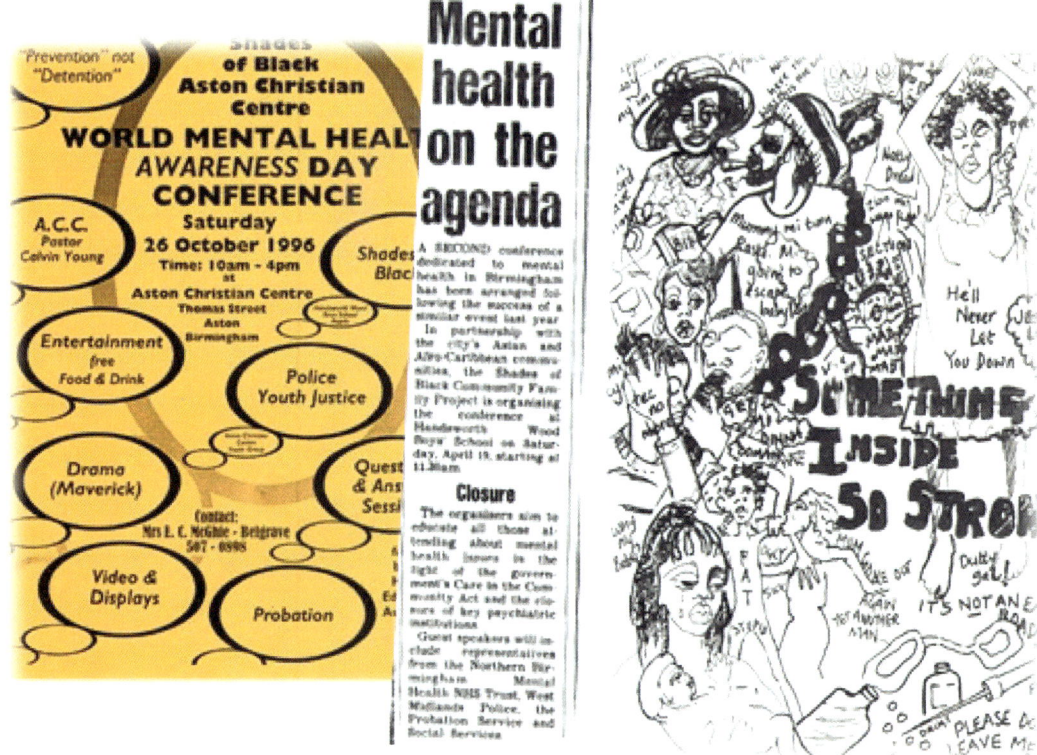

Shades of Black Community Family Project

The project brought families together by organising cultural and social activities for each age group. These included conferences, lectures, trips, and artwork, holiday schemes especially for children and garden parties and dinners for the elderly. I was also able to assist in student assignment work through colleges and universities. I was also offered promotion but I declined this as I wanted to continue working in the community.

The Shades of Black Community Family Project was established in 1989 within the the work I did with the Probation Aftercare Service.

In the summer of 1985, there was a period of high unemployment in Birmingham and the young people of Handsworth were caught up in a situation where there was anger and hostility against the state, which resulted in what has become known as the Handsworth riots, where both private and commercial buildings were burnt.

After the riot, a number of neighbourhood and community projects sprang up to reassure, reconcile and rebuild.

During 1989, it became apparent a number of Afro-Caribbean people were experiencing some form of stress or stress-related symptoms which showed themselves among the young, middle-aged and elderly. This showed me there was a need to examine the problem closely and to seek ways and means to help alleviate or minimise the problem.

At grass roots level, what happened next was a remarkable journey of courage and reconciliation, reassurance and rebuilding of lives. My friends believed I was capable to be the appropriate leader after the aftermath of the Handsworth riots in 1985, to assist in the process of reconciliation, reassurance and rebuilding people's lives. After accepting the challenge, the first meeting was held at the community Probation Service centre.

In our first meeting took place in the winter of 1988. It was found that stress amongst the young people aged between 16-30 years was through unemployment and low academic attainment, which brought frustration and usually leads to some form of mental disorder.

Both the middle-aged and elderly appear to suffer from a similar stress-related problem, i.e. living alone, incapacitated by either arthritis, partial sight, stroke (palsy), or some form of mental disorder, and quite often these sufferers do not have any visitors.

It was decided to organise a group of sufferers with stress or stress-related problems with a view that, through social interactions and recreational activities, it would lift their spirits and enhance their self-esteem. At our first meeting, 30 adults came for a coffee morning visit to the Probation Aftercare Centre. Out of this, Shades of Black Community Family Project came into being on 1st February, 1989.

A voluntary Committee of Management of five ladies, including myself, was set up to steer the new group and consider strategies and a programme of activities which would eventually lead us to our goals. Programmes of activities were arranged on Saturdays for senior citizens and children of all ages.

The committee clarified aims and objectives and a formal constitution was drawn up. Shades of Black Community Family Project was not only black participants engaging in the management of the project, because white individuals were also involved. We had roles and responsibilities and met the first Monday of every month. We progressed a mission statement, and constitution CRB checks of children welfare policies were organised

After months of planning, the managerial launch for Shades of Black took place on 26th August 1989 at The Cultural Centre, 326/328 Hamstead Road, Handsworth. With the skills and expertise of the Committee of Management and personal contact, 30 people attended the inaugural launch. To facilitate administrative costs, a token subscription was encouraged, and members have a sense of belonging when they have needed a contribution. Subscription also forms a part of fund-raising.

In addition to the main work of the Committee of Management, it is gratifying to include the invaluable help of volunteers from members of the community, including the local police, fire service, girls from the local schools, St John's Ambulance Brigade, The West Midlands Probation Aftercare Organisation, University of Central England, North Birmingham College and City Council. It may be well documented that Shades of Black is a community family project for the community, a programme for pleasure and community involvement.

By 1990, 25 volunteers were registered to assist in the programmes of activities and debates about racism between black immigrants and white people, and how we would be able to rebuild people's lives after the 1985 Handsworth riots.

As Shades of Black volunteers, we planned family basic life skills programmes of activities and have been an inspirational educational asset at grass roots level for thousands of individuals between 1989 to 2019 I have been the lynchpin of the project's operation, and co-ordinator for the past 30 years.

Working together from 1989 was a magnificent opportunity for educational experiences. The legacy of the Shades of Black Community Family Project will always live on. It's the simplest way in which the project is always presented to all. After 25 years, the project delivery service is still uniquely strong. In order to secure Shades of Black's hard work for others, the project information is documented, and most of the information is place in central library archives for basic life skills educational learning since 2011. Shades of Black Community Family Project has excelled in inspiring social activities and programme achievements since their inception in 1989. We have received several high-profile awards, especially two from Her Majesty Queen Elizabeth II.

After 40 years of working in Handsworth with my family and friends in several local projects, I was approached by one of my street neighbours to manage an elderly social group. The purpose was to get together to discuss concerns about the needs of others. Shades of Black Community Family Project is non-sectarian and non-political, with the diversity and religious faith which the new immigrants brought with them from the land of their birth; religious tolerance and harmony is encouraged. Topical issues and current affairs are aired without prejudice or political bias.

I designed good housekeeping and independent living programmes which concentrated upon elements of personal hygiene, cookery, budgeting and general basic domestic life skills, thereby enhancing those qualities of self-respect normally associated with a less delinquent lifestyle.

The little things in life are often neglected, but isn't it those little things which prove so essential to our sense of well-being and self-respect? How often have we witnessed individuals and clients who seem to be caught up into a downward spiral,

where offending became one example of an extreme disregard for even their own personal welfare. For most individuals and offenders, a stable domestic basic domestic lifestyle would seem to be a pre-requisite in their avoidance of further offending, but this does not merely mean the possession of accommodation alone, an increasingly elusive objectives in itself. After all, there is a difference between a house and a home.

HELP and SIGNS projects

Following the exemplary legacy of my ancestors, Shades of Black committee volunteer members felt some responsibilities towards the sustainability of the soil and environmental issues.

The creation of the Help Enables Learning Positively "HELP" and the Social Inclusion Greenland Nurturing Scheme "SIGNS" Curriculum Allotment Garden Project was an environmental initiative through Shades of Black working and funding partners. It provides access to basic life skills learning for local school pupils and the local community.

To encourage local school pupils and staff and the wider community to be involved, this learning gets young people and senior citizens to interact.

The teaching/learning experience provided an essential well-being opportunity for those interested in healthy living. Fresh vegetables were planted, watered, harvested and cooked as a part of our daily meals. The HELP/SIGNS Project could easily be integrated into a government healthy eating campaign.

The HELP/SIGNS Project started with eight pupils from Handsworth Wood Girls' School. Since then, several other local schools, nurseries and the community of Handsworth and Stechford worked on the project.

From March to November each year, over 12 schools and three nurseries were involved with approximately 300 pupils working between three to five days per week in two shifts. We delivered one-and-a-half hour lessons on the allotment sites in Handsworth and Stechford, Shades of Black was awarded the Queen's Golden

Jubilee Award for Voluntary service in 2004. Our hard work in creating projects for the involvement, development and participation of the local multi-cultural wider society gained us several awards including a Pride of Britain Award, the BBC WM Award 2012, WRVS Award in 2011 and several others.

Our collaborative involvement with Seed Organic from Ryton Organic Gardens in Coventry resulted in a meeting with HRH the Prince of Wales and the television presenter James Yong took place on July 14th 2011 and August 20th 2011.

Because of funding criteria the HELP project name was changed to SIGNS project in 2007.

]HELP-SIGNS allotment project since 2008-2013 was moved to Stechford Village Francis Road Allotment, Birmingham. The project co-ordinator continued to present basic life skills to local school pupils, teachers and the wider local community.

Funded by Yardley and community funds from 2008-2012, there are two primary schools, Stechford Primary and Corpus Christi, working on the project. This is an opportunity where emphasis is placed on programme plans, healthy living and eating, basic lifestyle skills, an educational learning curve for pupils, teachers and adults at grass roots levels. They had also received awards from the Evening Mail for the positive participation with the HELP/SIGNS allotment project.

Since 1993, I became a resident in Stechford village, an extension of the Shades of Black work. I also became a member of Stechford Village Community Forum, because of my involvements in Bulks street and home rubbish collection. Free smoke alarms were given to seniors and also security gates for the protection of all citizens. This is just some of the work that Shades of Black was involved with in Handsworth. I also became a member of Stechford Baptist Church in Victoria Road. A church garden was also started, and vegetables, fruits, flowers were presented at the harvest church service and shared with members.

Pictured above, Uplands allotment,
below, Home-based Educational Learning Garden Project

In October 2010 I was invited to Probation service black history "Now and Then Project." It was very nice to be able to pay a return visit to the very building where Shades of Black had originated and excels over 22 years both in work and volunteering position for the last 25 years of my working life, what takes approximately years where the developments of a unique prestigious programme of activities for basic educational skills were an invaluable part of service delivery for offending client involvement development with the Probation Service.

It is a pleasure to be endorsed by Carl Morgan of the probation service here is his written quotation, written by Carl Morgan: E*unice gave a presentation about her experiences as a black woman volunteering in probation for over 25 years, getting a MBE from the Queen, the pride of meeting the Queen again to receive the Queen Jubilee Award and the "Real" pride of working with young people and offenders across the boundaries of Handsworth, Aston and Stechford areas of Birmingham.*

Mrs McGhie-Belgrave founder of the Shades of Black Community Family Project with loyal volunteers committee members, introduced the Help Enables Learning Positively Signs Social Inclusion Greenland Nurturing Scheme Project Basic Educational life skills in gardening in 1998 at the Uplands allotments in Birmingham.

This was primarily for local primary and secondary school teachers/pupils, and also the wider multi-cultural community access the boundaries of Handsworth and Stechford in Birmingham.

With the Shades of Black project, excellent service delivery is our inspirational aim. We want all users of our service to enjoy the Best ISA (Best Education Structured Training in Sewing Art Project), where parents and local people learn how to sew their own clothes and school uniforms, where Asian and Muslim parents are participating and developing their skills. We also received a letter from Her Majesty Queen Elizabeth II for our work in 2012

Best ISA Sewing

The Best Education Structure Training In Sewing Art (BEST ISA) started in Handsworth Wood Girls' School with 6th form pupils, in 2000-2004 the Shades of Black Community Family Project co-ordinator Mrs McGhie-Belgrave MBE and school governor. Pupils work was also presented in Soho through House Museum to the multi-cultural local wider community as an educational learning school curriculum sewing programme activity. when cushions/costumes were made and presented to the wider public in Soho House Museum for a long time.

The BEST ISA was also delivered to parents and pupils as education learning experiences at Stechford Primary School and others. It was a **unique sewing project for Asian parents and pupils in an educational capacity whilst they learnt basic English and enjoyed companionship for two hours on Mondays and Tuesdays from 2008-13 at Stechford Primary School.**

The work that has been accomplished through the World War I cenotaph memorial in Stechford. Embroidery relating to the services held and wreaths laid through special service delivery to the research war project by pupils of Stechford Primary School since 2007.

The school involvement started in 2005 in the *Changing Taste of Food* programme which was shown on Channel Four Television.

Stechford Primary School has been very actively engaged in Shades of Black. My thanks to all at the schools for your help and assistance, especially in the shared space for parents BEST ISA sewing project, which is growing in numbers all the time in the Stechford area, and pupils' involvement in the allotment garden project at Francis Road allotments.

Stechford Primary School pupils and teaching staff between 2008-2014 assisted Shades of Black in the successful growing and harvest of fresh vegetables. They also managed to arrange an enterprising sale in the school hall to purchase seeds for the sowing and planting season. Corpus Christi Primary School pupils and teaching staff have supported us at the allotment plot site, where various organisations e.g. the organic Ryton Garden and student photographers visited. All will be pleased to know that the student from Birmingham University had a distinction in his examination as a journalist. Thank you all for helping Shades of Black help others when you can.

Skills for Community Work

"My Grandma Didn't Teach Me to Read for Nothing."

Communications and Publicity

Communication skills are an essential factor in Shades of Black operation, such as a personal contact liaison with other community organisations, both statutory and voluntary (networking), contacting the different local churches and schools.

I felt very proud that my poor family in Jamaica educated me throughout my childhood and teenage years, I, in turn, have involved my grandchildren in my work and I have helped them to develop their writing and creative skills as well as good manners and how to communicate with others effectively

Publicity has been a critical factor in the success of our projects and a contributor to us gaining multiple awards, the awards in themselves bring more publicity

Publicity is also a high point communication skill through press, radio, television and handouts and booklets with the information set out clearly and, of course, personal contact. Publicity was also obtained through the local and National newspapers, radio and television.

(See examples in Gallery on page)

Wednesday 18th August 2009
My Allotment Poem
Today I went to the allotment,
I go there every week,
I like planting carrots, parsnips
and maybe some leek.

I sprinkle some seeds
And pulled out loads of weeds
After lunch,
I got going,
did some heavy digging and seed sowing.

It was really warm,
With the beautiful yellow corn,
And the rest of the flowers,
Started growing for hours.

-Written by my grand daughter in 2009

Fundraising

Money is the lifeblood of every organisation, and this is equally true of Shades of Black. Administrative costs, materials for special projects outdoors and indoors, and recreational activities are included in the financial strategy. So a fund-raising scheme was set up to facilitate the programme of activities, schemes such as raffles, tombolas, members and friends sale of work. Shades of Black are indebted to charities and friends who supported the family project with grants and donations.

The fund-raising process was through the Probation Aftercare Service and wider local community, presenting gifts for raffling, and yearly subscriptions and also financial help from Probation.

We raised funds through events and activities, the Easter parade project for parent/children from the local community. Other projects are a fund-raising fashion show, Christmas dinners for senior citizens. Exhibition in local museums, libraries, churches, schools and other public buildings in Handsworth, and the BEST ISA sewing project 2000-2004 in Handsworth Girls' school, Stechford Primary School in 2009-2014.

In the 1960s, I had no funding for community action work within the wider local multi-cultural community. All the projects and activities programmes have been funded by several funders since February 1989. The Big Lottery Fund and Heritage Lottery award funds are the largest subscribers towards the dynamic, unique community family project. There are also other funders, including Interserve building contractors and Shell Better Britain. Other awards, approximately 17, were gained through the work accomplished and are: Black Mental Health Research project for two years, Awareness in HIV debatable issues involvement research Black, Asian and White the commonwealth World War I and II project pupils and teachers input, HELP enables Learning Positively started in 1998 and SIGNS Social Inclusion Greenland Nurturing Scheme allotment project started 2004, Learning about healthy living basic gardening skills,

In return, transparent documentation had to be developed in photo albums and written booklet documentation form, with both pupils and Shades of Black community's memories of duration of project between one year to three years and sometimes a much longer period. All committee members had participated in several other project programmes. All the projects presented are educational and inspirational to thousands of individuals.

Pupils from Stechford Primary School learning basic life skills at Francis Road allotment

Uplands Allotment with a few children on exchange from Holland

Uplands Allotment

Interview outside my home with Carl Chinn MBE

Taken at Soho House Handsworth

Awards & Accolades

Mrs Eunice Cynthia McGhie-Belgrave MBE

Our First Award

JRH/DWW

9 March 1990

Mrs E.C. McGhie,
36, Herbert Road,
Handsworth,
Birmingham

Dear Mrs McGhie,

Congratulations - you have been awarded a Mercury Care Medal which is enclosed.

The Medal was awarded to you for your care and consideration for others.

In a world in which we are constantly being told that "no one cares" it gives me great pleasure to know that there are so many like yourself who put others first.

Of course, people do care about others and it was with this thought that we launched the Medal award scheme.

It is an alternative honours scheme which I hope will become annual and which recognises the work carried out by people who are not catered for in traditional honours lists.

So well done, and wear your Medal with pride.

Yours sincerely,

Joe Holmes,
Acting Editor.

The Birmingham Post & Mail Ltd

Learning and Growing. A lifetime of Service by God's Grace

Member of The Most Excellent Order of The British Empire (M.B.E)

Mrs Eunice Cynthia McGhie-Belgrave MBE

Learning and Growing. A lifetime of Service by God's Grace

Mrs Eunice Cynthia McGhie-Belgrave MBE

Learning and Growing. A lifetime of Service by God's Grace

Mrs Eunice Cynthia McGhie-Belgrave MBE

The Queens Golden Jubilee Award

Mrs. E C McGhie-Belgrave MBE and Mrs. S Hyman outside St. James Palace Monday July 19th 2004 6:30pm- 8:30pm to reception given by the Queen and The Duke of Edinburgh as winners of The Queen's Golden Jubilee Awards for Unsung Heroes Voluntary Service 2004.

HIGHGROVE

His Royal Highness The Prince of Wales
requests the pleasure of the company of

Mrs Eunice McGhie-Belgrave

at a Reception at Highgrove for Garden Organic
on Thursday, 14th July 2011

Pour Mémoire

Time: 4.30pm
Dress: Lounge Suit

Citizenship Award for Diversity

Gallery

HANDSWORTH: Young and old at fire station harvest festival

■ BURNING AMBITION... Eunice McGhie-Belgrave MBE vowed to organise the first harvest festival in a fire station

Eunice's ideas bearing fruit!

By Poppy Brady

GREEN-fingered youngsters in Birmingham blazed a trail by holding a harvest festival of their produce in their local community fire station.

The event was held for the first time at Handsworth's community fire station and involved youngsters from several primary schools and Handsworth Wood Girls School.

The woman behind the event [is] grandmother Eunice McGhie-Belgrave, MBE who set up pioneer project Shades of Black more than 30 years ago.

Her scheme expanded to include encouraging youngsters to grow their own food on Europe's largest allotment site at Uplands, in Oxhill Road.

"The allotments project has simply [begun a] cycle of healthy eating for everyone.

Youngsters from Wattville Primary School and Rookery Primary School were at the harvest festival yesterday along with elderly residents.

Handsworth fire safety centre manager Tim Smyth said: "I think this is unique – I haven't heard of a fire station hosting a harvest festival before."

Eunice's new fight

Campaigner takes on rail network

By Poppy Brady

VETERAN CAMPAIGNER Eunice McGhie-Belgrave is taking on the might of Birmingham's rail network in her latest campaign to improve access to Stechford Station.

The indomitable grandmother wants proper levelled access to Stechford Station, which she said is currently impossible to traverse for anyone using a wheelchair or a pushchair.

Mrs McGhie-Belgrave, who set up the Shades of Black community project in Handsworth following riots in the 1980s, sought to describe the situation: "Stechford Station is only seven minutes from Birmingham city centre but so many people can't use it because there are 72 steps to climb before you reach the platform. The bus, on the other hand takes around 45 minutes.

Youngsters from Stechford Primary School and Corpus Christ Catholic Primary have collected scores of names in a petition which has now been presented to Birmingham Yardley, Lib Dem MP John Hemming.

In explaining the support of school children, she said, 'Local youngsters have got

LOOKING FOR IMPROVEMENTS: Mrs Eunice McGhie-Belgrave with MP John Hemming (left) and Stechford Lib-Dem Councillor Neil Eustace

improve the station because they see so many people who simply can't use it. They feel something needs to be done."

Birmingham Yardley Lib-Dem MP John Hemming, who received the petition, said in response that "this is an excellent station and almost 300,000 people a year use it but a lot more would use it if it had better level access. I intend to take this issue to Transport Minister Norman Baker."

Hemming pointed out that "the previous Government invested money improving the rail network in the south east.

investment."

Chris Mepham, of London Midland Rail Network, expressed sympathy at the concerns but said there was a lack of funds to undertake the necessary improvement works. "We are sympathetic to everyone's concerns about access but there is a limited pot of money," he said, adding that "to improve access by extending the footbridge and installing a lift would probably cost around a million pounds."

He, however, said the rail company was "committed to looking at ways of improving the

"Community Unites for Positive Mental Health Care Change"

by Veron Graham

AROUND 150 community people attended a conference promoting mental health awareness in Aston, Birmingham in October.

The "Prevention not Detention" conference was held at Aston Christian Centre in Thomas Street and was funded by the Health Education Authority. It aimed to educate the public on issues of mental health and ease fears resulting from the Government's recently introduced 'Care in the Community' programme. The programme aims to treat some of the ill in their homes instead of admitting them to institutions.

Professionals were on hand to inform and answer questions from the majority Black audience, which included mentally ill outpatients.

There was also deep concern about the over-representation of Black people in the mental health system. Professor Max Birchwood representing the Trust's Northern Birmingham department commented: "The high rate of detention among Blacks is a sign that they are receiving help too late. Providing early treatment for the mentally ill is crucial. However it can take up to two years after symptoms start to develop before many receive effective treatment. There is a deep Black mistrust of psychiatric care."

Heated debate was prompted over Police treatment of ill offenders. West Midland Police Inspector Tim Godwin responded: "The police station is not the best place to take the mentally ill, but at present we are the only ones who can lawfully apprehend such a person."

Professor Birchwood is in charge of the Early Psychosis Centre in the Birmingham city centre. Their objective is to detect and care for people in the early stages of illness and so help to prevent the need for detention in mental hospitals. "I have been heartened by the influence of community groups on Government policy but there is still some way to go," he continued.

Professor Max Birchwood addresses the conference.

Inspector Tim Godwin greets conference organiser Eunice McGhie.

Liaison Probation Officer Viv Thompson who handles cases of the mentally ill who pass through the criminal justice system approved of the day's events and said: 'Information is power and if knowledge is shared with the public we can go up and challenge the professionals in the areas of policy making.

The conference was organised by Eunice McGhie-Belgrave - secretary of 'Shades of Black' a voluntary self-help project based in Handsworth, Birmingham - at the request of community people and care reformers.

Mrs. McGhie's work and commitment has made her a finalist for the TSB annual 'Citizenship Award' to be presented in November (see article entitled 'Community Activist to be Citizen of the Year?'). She added: "Authorities are trying to help but many in the community do not understand mental illness and need to be more aware."

Shades of Black were very happy with the proceedings and announced plans to hold a similar event in April 1997.

■ GREENS PARTY: Pupils gardeners of Handsworth Wood Girls School, from the left, Vicki Holden (12), Zoe Crawford (12), Maria Blair (12) and Mandeep Dilbeher (12)

The veggie brigade!

Report by Poppy Brady

Pupils get dug in for OAPs

DIG this! Green fingered pupils in Birmingham are giving goodie bags of food to local old folk, made up of vegetables they have grown themselves.

Budding gardeners at Handsworth Wood Girls School are scooping bumper crops of winter vegetables at the plots they tend on the nearby Uplands Allotments site.

Now, elderly residents living near the school in Church Lane are reaping the benefit of the pupils' hard work and have received bags of potatoes, pumpkins, spinach and cabbage.

The pioneering allotments project, which is the only one of its kind in the city, was launched more than two years ago and is funded by the Shell Better Britain Campaign and Birmingham City Council.

It is also supported by Shades of Black, a which has introduced the girls to their first ta of gardening. Head teacher Dr Stephen Nepa ingh said: "We're very proud of the girls becau many have never done any gardening before. fact they've just won a prize for growing the b spinach at Uplands which is one of the bigg allotments in the country.

"We have two plots, but now we're hoping f third because several local primary schools want to join us."

Writing reports

He added: "We are certainly not taking the dren away from their lessons because they in porate the gardening into the curriculum by wri reports, taking videos and photographs and i acting with the community."

Mandeep Dilbeher, aged 12, who is among a of 24 students who tend the plots once a week. "It's great fun - even when it's raining I'd never any gardening before, but when I'm older I'd li have my own plot."

Learning and Growing. A lifetime of Service by God's Grace

PROVIDING FOOD FOR THOUGHT

Veteran uniting people across all boundaries

By Poppy Brady

BACK IN THE DAY: Black and white photo of Mrs McGhie launching Shades of Black in 1989.

PROUD MOMENT: Mrs McGhie-Belgrave receiving her Pride of Britain award from comedian Lenny Henry

THE ROOTING that has recently scarred Birmingham will re-ignite with grandmother Eunice McGhie-Belgrave, who was a pioneer during similar troubles in the city more than two decades ago.

Determined to stop what she described as the "restlessness" ruining her community all those years ago, Mrs McGhie launched a project called Shades of Black to bring people together.

That was in 1989 and Shades of Black is possibly one of the only schemes launched to unite a fractured community in the wake of the 1980s riots that still thrives in Birmingham today.

Her straightforward style and simple, practical ideas have stood the test of time and united people across all boundaries – and now at 77, Mrs McGhie, as she is known to generations of youngsters, is showing no signs of slowing down.

"What has happened here again in Birmingham has made me very sad, but we have to pick ourselves up and carry on," says Mrs McGhie, who has amassed countless awards over the years in recognition of her work including an MBE and a Pride of Britain award in 2009.

The Shades of Black Community Family Project was originally launched to enhance the life skills of a multi-racial community, promoting social activities at grass-roots level. Youngsters were taught the basics duced to simple vegetable growing on local allotments.

"I was horrified at how little youngsters seemed to know about growing food. Many had never seen fresh vegetables," explained Mrs McGhie, who left her beloved St James in Jamaica to arrive in a cold Britain in February 1957. Sadly, she has never returned to her homeland.

GROWING

What started with pupils from Handsworth Wood Girls' School on plots at Uplands Allotments, spread to many schools across Handsworth Soon, hundreds of pupils were learning the basics of growing and cooking their own food.

"I'm pleased that it's a skill which has stayed with them all their lives," says Mrs McGhie, who moved her allotment project to Frances Road nearer her home in Stechford in 1993 when the journeying to Handsworth became too much.

"I often meet some of the original youngsters who are now grown up with children of their own. But they always said they to grow and cook food."

And the scheme also cuts across the generations as local elderly are always given boxes of fresh vegetables grown by the youngsters at harvest time.

Featured on BBC's Gardener's World, the project was seen as a trailblazer for other communities across the UK. It even passes on gardening skills to young offenders – from clearing land for planting right through to eating the end results.

Not content with just Shades of Black, Mrs McGhie launched the Commonwealth World War I and World War II Black, White and Asian Veterans Research Project in Stechford with help from the Heritage Lottery Fund in 2007.

Again, it's united the community with more than 200 pupils from Corpus Christi and Stechford primary schools taking part in a special service of remembrance at Stechford cenotaph.

With research help from volunteers, it gave many youngsters a chance to understand their roots and how their grandfathers' generation made the ultimate sacrifice.

Mrs McGhie is still just as passionate about her gardening and still spends most days tending the quarter of an acre she now runs at Stechford allotments where youngsters come to learn.

She puts her long healthy life down to "plenty of fresh air" but says her parents instilled in her a discipline that has stayed with her all her life.

"From the age of three I could face the public," she says. "We had to read the Bible scriptures in church. It was all about communication and I got all that from

---

Grandmother works to make sure soldiers not forgotten

By Poppy Brady

GRANDMOTHER EUNICE McGhie-Belgrave has worked tirelessly for years to make sure the younger generation in her Birmingham community never forget those who made the ultimate sacrifice.

Like the war memorial that unites five streets in Stechford, Eunice with her Shades of Black community group, got local people together to research the history behind the memorial.

Now scores of youngsters from two local schools – Corpus Christi Catholic Primary and Stechford Primary – honour the area's war dead each Remembrance Day.

With help from a Heritage Lottery Award, Eunice launched a research project into the veterans of World War One and Two, wanting to learn more about the 51 soldiers whose names grace the Stechford cenotaph which stands at the central point of five main roads in the area.

In a service led by Rev Griphus Gakuru, vicar of All Saints church, youngsters laid wreaths of poppies in the third annual ceremony. An extra plaque, financed by the Community Chest Fund, to honour those who gave their lives in war, was also unveiled.

Eunice, who launched Shades of Black in Birmingham following inner-city unrest during the 1980s, said: "It's so important that the next generation never forgets those who gave their tomorrows for our today. The children get so much from researching the history of the cenotaph. They learn about their roots and how their grandfathers' generation paid the ultimate price."

HISTORY: Eunice McGhie-Belgrave and local youngsters lay wreaths at Stechford cenotaph

CLARENCE HOUSE
LONDON SW1A 1BA

From: The Office of TRH The Prince of Wales and The Duchess of Cornwall

PRIVATE AND CONFIDENTIAL

26th August, 2011

Dear Mrs. McGhie-Belgrave,

The Prince of Wales has asked me to thank you for your recent letter and for very kindly sending a copy of 'The Commonwealth World War I and World War II Black, White and Asian Veterans Research Project.'

The speech that you gave at Highgrove was most inspiring, as indeed is all the tireless work that you do. His Royal Highness wishes you continued success in the future.

This comes with His Royal Highness's warmest thanks and best wishes.

Yours sincerely,

Olivia Morrell

Mrs. E C McGhie-Belgrave MBE

Children pay respects

HUNDREDS of Birmingham children lined the streets to pay their respects to soldiers killed since the First World War.

Pupils from Stechford Primary School and Corpus Christi Catholic Primary School laid poppy wreaths at a war memorial outside their schools.

The children have been working on a two-year research project to find out more about the soldiers named on the cenotaph.

They were given a £47,000 Heritage Lottery Fund grant to visit London and France to trace the men.

Eunice Belgrave, a community worker for the Shades of Black project, said: "The children really enjoyed finding out about their history and the two world wars.

"They went to London to look at the National Archives and have even been to France to visit the graves of local soldiers. Yesterday they stood by the war memorial to pay their respects in a two-minute silence."

The community project was to end next month but a group of mums have vowed to keep it going into next year.

Silent: Iqia Ishakeel and fellow Year 6 pupils of Stechford Primary School pay their respects on Armistice Day.

Mrs Eunice Cynthia McGhie-Belgrave MBE

HERO EUNICE

OUR Unsung Hero awards are aimed at recognising staff who go the extra mile to help customers and colleagues.

But we've made an exception this month, by awarding the title to an ex-employee – 70-year-old Eunice McGhie-Belgrave MBE. Eunice, who used to work as a cook in social services, gets her award for her tireless drive to change lives, which means she works closely with Education and Leisure.

She was nominated by William Stephens from Shades of Black, the council-backed group she helped set up after the Handsworth riots, and granddaughter Melissa, who saw Inner Voice at school.

Eunice said: "Our HELP initiative – it stands for Help Enables Learning Positively – started on the Uplands allotment in Handsworth in 1998 and has been a soaraway success.

"With help from the parks and nature conservation team, we started with eight pupils. We've now got seven schools and 215 kids on board, from tots to teenagers, with three allotments, a school garden and church land.

"The youngsters are learning life skills like caring for wildlife, growing herbs and vegetables from seed, weeding, watering and harvesting, as well as photography and video-making.

● Digging in – Unsung Hero Eunice McGhie-Belgrave and granddaughter Melissa

have even held cookery demonstrations at the Birmingham College of Food, Creative Studies and Tourism."

For more information, call Eunice on 07702 919 169.

● If you would like to nominate a colleague as an unsung hero, call Mary Munford on 303 4665 or e-mail Inner Voice via Lotus Notes or at inner.voice@birmingham.gov.uk

Learning and Growing. A lifetime of Service by God's Grace

Queen voluntary awards presented by Lord mayor and Admiral

111

ALLOTMENT life
Back to school

How do you get kids into gardening? **Jane Moore** discovers an inner-city allotment project that helps schools do just that. Photos by Nick Smith

Do you remember how you first got the gardening bug? For many of us, it was sowing a few seeds at a tender age with a green-fingered parent. It's our responsibility, as adults, to pass on our growing skills to the next generation.

This is easier said than done with children from city centres – they often live in flats where the only green outdoor space is the local park. Some kids might be lucky enough to have parents or grandparents with an allotment, but many more are less fortunate.

Sonia Hyman, chair of the Shades of Black project in Birmingham, has spent the past 10 years introducing city children to the messy, muddy, munchable world of gardening. "When we started the project there were just two of us and we were determined to make a difference to the kids here," Sonia says. "After the Handsworth riots, everything seemed so bleak and we wanted to do something positive."

The project was set up specifically to get inner-city kids involved with growing, harvesting and learning about vegetables in the hope that their gardening skills and confidence levels would improve. By working with local schools at infant, primary and secondary levels, the Shades of Black project has also improved relations within the local community, as well as shedding a more positive light on the Handsworth area, forever associated with race riots in the 1980s.

"The heads of the schools we work with realise that it does the children a lot of good," says Eunice McGhie-Belgrave OBE, the project founder.

"It's gone from strength to strength as people have recognised the new skills and confidence that growing things gives young people."

Different school groups visit Shades of Black each week and learn how to sow, grow, water, weed and harvest. The three linked plots are filled with cabbages, carrots, pumpkins and sunflowers, as well as some more exotic crops, such as callaloo, which reflect the ethnic diversity of the Handsworth schoolchildren.

There's also a small orchard and a simple seating area of log stools and benches which serves as an outdoor classroom. "A lot of the children don't have gardens at home and have no experience of gardening," says Jo Wedderburn, a teacher at Rookery Road School in Birmingham, one of the schools involved in the

TV BAD BOYS ARE PUTTY IN MY HANDS

By Vicky Farncombe
STAFF REPORTER

THEY are known for terrifying contestants on their TV shows with their brutal honesty and sarcastic put-downs.

But Simon Cowell and Gordon Ramsay are no match for 75-year-old Eunice McGhie-Belgrave MBE. The devoted community worker who was handed a Pride of Britain award last year for inspiring hundreds of children to grow their own vegetables thinks they're a pair of pussy cats.

In October, the *Birmingham Mail* revealed that Mrs McGhie-Belgrave had approached Simon to make a record with the youngsters she helps.

Now she's persuaded foulmouthed Gordon Ramsay to stump up the cash for a board game that will teach children and parents about healthy eating.

"If you don't ask, you don't get," said great grandmother Eunice, who lives in Stechford. "They can only say no.

"I asked Gordon about funding the board game when he presented me with my Pride of Britain award.

"He wanted to give me the cash right then and there but I told him I'd send him the details first.

"He's given me an unconditional yes."

Eunice is enlisting the help of schoolchildren in Birmingham to devise and name the board game which will be centred around identifying fruit, vegetables and herbs.

"I want to mass market the board game. I want it in every toy shop," said Eunice.

Money from the venture will be used to enable more youngsters to garden at the Shades of Black allotments, in Handsworth and Stechford.

Shades of Black was formed in 1985 to heal and unite Handsworth following the riots which devastated the area.

"When I first started out in 1989 people laughed at me and said it wouldn't work," said Eunice.

"Growing vegetables seems simple and it is.

"It teaches kids a healthy lifestyle. Not all children are good in a classroom so this gives them an opportunity to shine in a different way."

Ramsay said he was in awe of the super gran. "It is extraordinary what she has done," he said.

The 'First Lady of allotments' is still waiting for a reply from Cowell after she collared him at the Pride of Britian awards ceremony.

"I've written him a letter and I'm hoping to hear from him soon," she said.

Jamaican-born Eunice revealed her dealings with the stars yesterday at the press launch of the UK's first ever Edible Garden Show. The national show to celebrate the work of gardeners who grow their own fruit and veg will be staged at Stoneleigh Park, in Warwickshire, from March 19 to 21.

"I'm delighted to support this fantastic new event," said Eunice, who was joined by children from Rookery Primary School.

'Pussy cat': Gordon Ramsay

IN A CLASS OF THEIR OWN

...ils from three local schools enjoy the prospect of a day at Uplands ...otments. Children have been gardening here since 1998 when ...minent local community leader and school governor Mrs McGee ...rted to bring children one morning a week to the plots. ...upported by a large oil company and the local Council, which are continuing to support the successful and increasingly popular scheme, Mrs McGee has been able to buy seed, wellingtons, overalls, tools and two sheds for the children. All those taking part seem to have enjoyed the whole process, with teachers reporting improvements in children's behaviour and performan...

SOB VOLUNTEERS

gham.co.uk/mail/news/centralcity   Monday 24th October 2005

HANDSWORTH: Youngsters hand out veg to elderly

Pupils give it a grow!

■ GREEN DAY... Daphne Powell, of Edgbaston, with (from left) top: Charniquoi Stanley, Rajdeep Chana and Maria Nawaz. Bottom: Hugh Jenkins and Sonia Dhesi.   Picture: Alan Williams

By Poppy Brady

GROWING, growing, gone! Scores of green-fingered youngsters have given local elderly folk heaps of fresh vegetables that they have grown themselves.

The pupils' seventh annual harvest festival at Handsworth's Uplands Allotments, in Oxhill Road, saw children from six local schools giving produce to the elderly.

The scheme was set up by Eunice McGhie-Belgrave MBE, who chairs the Shades of Black community family group based in Handsworth. She has always stressed the importance of showing young people how to grow and cook food from scratch rather than relying on convenience meals.

Her pioneering project has paid off as the allotment scheme has mushroomed. Erdington-based building contractors Inter-Serve have also helped to divide up plots, paint sheds, build new compost boxes and are now planning to create a new toilet block on the site.

Youngsters from Rookery, Foundry, Grove Lane and Wilkes Green Primary Schools, Handsworth Wood Girls' School and St John Wall School all took part. More than 25 senior citizens were given hampers of vegetables which also included sugar and packets of tea.

"It's a wonderful project that gets better every year," said Mrs McGhie-Belgrave. "The youngsters know how to grow anything from potatoes and onions to fresh herbs and pumpkins.

"It has made them realise that fresh vegetables grow in the ground, not on supermarket shelves. Now many of them want to cook what they have grown."

HANDSWORTH COMMUNITY FIRE SAFETY CENTRE GOES GREEN

It all started off as it usually does with a simple idea – "let's put some hanging baskets up to make the place look nice."

This was quickly followed by a suggestion that local groups could be invited to get involved, possibly children. Little could the team at Handsworth Community Fire Safety Centre have known how quickly the project would grow.

Centre Manager Tim Smyth was looking for people in the community to help with the project and was soon put in touch with Eunice McGhee-Belgrave and her friend Sonia Hyman.

They were founder members of the Shades of Black Project which had transformed overgrown land into allotments on Uplands Road in Handsworth. They have also been involved in a number of other community projects including Help Enables Learning Positively and Social Inclusion Greenland Nurturing Scheme.

Eunice has been awarded an MBE for her work for the community and has been to Buckingham Palace to meet the Queen on two occasions. She can also be seen on posters across the city promoting Handsworth

allotment and the centre's General Assistant Dave Evans was transformed into a horticulturalist overnight, earning the nickname Greenfingers in the process.

"There was a positive side to that, as we no longer had any problems locating him – he's in the allotment was the oft heard reply," commented Tim.

Over the summer the seeds grew into crops and members of staff and visitors to the centre were fascinated to see children working on the allotment.

step to extend that work to include fire safety messages and get the children to take them back to their homes.

This produce was harvested and presented to centre staff, visitors, children and parents

"Eunice has not stopped there," added Tim. "The woman is on a mission to turn the country green one plot at a time

"Greenfingers Evans turned into Carpenter Evans and set about building planting troughs for next

Central City News

HANDSWORTH: Children deliver festival treat for pensioners

Pupils' harvest blazes a trail

By Poppy Brady

PUPILS held a harvest festival with a difference with a visit to the fire station.

Youngsters from Wattville and Foundry primary schools treated pensioners at Handsworth community fire station to an array of fresh vegetables they planted and grew themselves.

Up to 25 boxes of healthy produce were handed out and another 10 were to be delivered to housebound old folk around Handsworth.

The vegetable scheme was organised at Uplands Allotments by the Shades of Black Family Project, founded by Eunice McGhie-Belgrave in the wake of the Handsworth riots more than 20 years ago.

She even set up a plot herself at the Rookery Road fire station, which she tends with the help of schoolchildren.

"The aim of the scheme is to give youngsters the knowledge and the power to start growing their own food at an early age," she said.

"Hopefully they will carry this on into adulthood and lay down good habits for life.

"With so much emphasis on obesity, I'm determined to help the next generation have as good a start as possible."

The allotments project involves up to half a dozen primary schools in Handsworth and Handsworth Wood Girls' School. The project owns at least two plots at the allotment site in Oxhill Road.

Handsworth fire station fire safety centre manager Tim Smyth said: "This was a great demonstration of the fire service's involvement with the local community."

■ HELMETFUL... Shernice Rai, 10, with deputy chief fire officer Vij Randeniya.

Mrs McGhie Belgrave
68 Victoria Road
Stechford
BIRMINGHAM
West Midlands B33 8AH

19 June 2018

Dear Mrs McGhie Belgrave

Thank you for your letter. We very much enjoyed reading the children's letters as well! It sounds like the work you do with Shades of Black is so amazing; it was lovely to read about it and see your brochure for the Community Garden Project.

Unfortunately, it's not possible to award a Green badge as Blue Peter Badges are only awarded to children aged 15 or under and to adults who appear on the programme. However, we would like to award you something for your hard work and care for your community, so we are enclosing a Blue Peter Cloth Emblem.

Thank you so much for writing to us, reading letters like these always makes us smile and brings a ray of sunshine into our day!

With best wishes from Lindsey, Radzi and all of us at Blue Peter

Yours sincerely

Ewan Vinnicombe
Editor
BLUE PETER

MY LEGACY

The legacy of the community work I pioneered will hopefully be an inspiration to many, to work hard as best you all can. If you do so, the results will be extraordinary.

There are artefacts, records and documentation about the inspirational local community volunteering action work that I have accomplished in the city museum and the new library in Birmingham. This includes written documentation, resources, photographs and some of the medals I have received.

"I grew up in Jamaica, my family served the community and that was instilled in me. I come to England and I served the community right from the beginning, all the way through."

TESTIMONIALS

Written by Mrs Sonia Hyman

It was in 1990 when I made a decision to join the Shades of Black Community Family Project based at Handsworth Probation Service building in Hamstead Road, Handsworth.

I have held several positions within the project and am still the Treasurer of these unique service delivery projects.

Mrs McGhie-Belgrave MBE and I, with the hard-working volunteers for many years, have been co-ordinators for all the projects within the Handsworth, Aston, Stechford and Small Heath areas of Birmingham.

When Shades of Black Project started, it was with Probation Aftercare Service providers in Birmingham to bring attention to local senior citizens' care e.g. visiting their homes, day trips to various locations, birthday parties for elders and young children. This was supported through fund-raising from the wider local community and probation services for approximately six years.

It was then we started the allotment project with funding from Shell Better Britain and Birmingham City Council for local schools and the wider local community children.

After two years' funding from Shell Better Britain and excellent outcomes, Shades of Black Community Family Project was able to access funding from the Millennium Awards seed lottery funding, Heritage Lottery funding, Community Fund action funding, The College of Food and others.

The work we've done includes HIV awareness, mental health projects, allotment projects, including the one at the largest site in Birmingham at Uplands Allotment for approximately 15 years with eight local secondary and primary schools in Birmingham. We also had nurseries and worked with disability organisations, churches, local residential homes, Soho Blakely Hall Museums and others. We also had international links with overseas visits.

In 2007, Shades of Black Project received £49,800 Heritage Lottery Funding for a World War I and World War II Black, White and Asians Research Project. The work is now presented in the new library archive along with other projects.

Written by Mr H Fuller
I arrived in England in the 1960s and Mrs Eunice McGhie was actively engaged in community action work in Handsworth for all, this is why I have no hesitation as to put in writing the contribution she has made towards the Shades of Black Community Family Project.

Mrs McGhie assisted in helping the senior citizens in every way possible, also the young children and housebound in several different ways; basic life skills and healthy eating is her special way of enhancing programmes of activities for all.

Everyone likes her simple ways of teaching and engaging individuals in work programme activities with the development of educational learning experiences for all.
The HELP Enables Learning Positively, Social Inclusion Greenland Nurturing Scheme, "Best Educational Structural Training Sewing Art, Railway Campaign for All, The home-based Learning Facilities Project and School Home.

Mrs McGhie-Belgrave has worked hard within the Shades of Black Community Family Projects. She has set several excellent examples for all to follow. That's why parents and their children have loved to participate in the Shades of Black Community Family Project Programme of Activities for the past 30 years.

Every year since 1919, Britain has honoured the war dead on November 11. The two-minute silence has become an inbuilt part of our national life. The blood-red poppy is a long-standing symbol of recognition of remembrance and commemoration. The first armistice, which concluded World War I in 1918, was signed at the 11th hour of the 11th day on the 11th month. One year later, in 1919, the silence was observed for the very first time. This poignant moment has been repeated every year since, not just in Britain, but many places around the world. Silence is observed at that specific moment, and in a way we remember all those who lost their lives in more recent conflicts.

The act of remembrance is not just something done out of respect and love, but rooted in tradition and dedication to pray for the dead. Praying for the dead is not morbid or unrealistic: it is beautiful, consoling, and important. In Stetchford, Birmingham, over recent years, the local community both young and old have gathered at the war memorial to observe Remembrance Day. Through Shades of Black spearheading, the two local schools – Corpus Christi and Stetchford Primary – bring pupils and staff to join with local community in marking this solemn moment.

The commonwealth World War I and World War II Veterans Heritage Lottery-funded project has a special dimension of contributing to life-long learning, whether that of school pupils or the wider community, in Stetchford and Handsworth areas of Birmingham. This reminds us that the war effort was universal across our country; every town and city took part. The war effort was one that was shared. Life histories have been recorded and these pieces of work are now invaluable.

The project itself has been practical in every way, and it has been fascinating to watch it evolve. People have been brought together from the whole community, with all sections involved and playing different parts. Pupils of Handsworth Wood Girls' School were so infused by working on the project that they put on a play – recreating and remembering in yet another way the importance of remembering those who gave their lives to shape our freedom today. But the special moments of the project do not stop there, for the legacy is ongoing. A celebration took place at Blakesley Hall that showcased the material the volunteers managed to unearth. In fact, the project has only scratched the surface: there are countless numbers of other veterans who remain waiting in the shadows to have their life histories brought to life.

More recently, to underscore the emphasis placed on life-long learning, collated material was presented to Birmingham Libraries and Archives, which is now available for future generations to benefit from. This project had developed and fostered greater social diversity cohesion. It is, therefore, only through honouring and adequately remembering the service of those who participated in the world wars that we can begin to develop a greater understanding of their contribution to society today – a contribution that is far too often overlooked.

I end this foreword by congratulating all those involved in the project for their immense efforts and contributions. Special thanks must go to Stetchford Primary School for making space available for a sewing room with embroidery activities for recreating some of the period costumes.

We must remember another underlying theme of the acts of remembrance, that of peace. Today, the absence of military conflict in our land is not peace. There is no true peace where injustice prevails. We should be mindful of the efforts we can make and encourage our political leaders to seek peace in international affairs. This ideal can be achieved in my lifetime, for it was freedom and liberty which our servicemen have fought and continue to fight for. For many people, remembrance is every day, not just on the 11th of November. We should be mindful of this.

Matthew T TYE BA Hons (Lond), MSc (Oxon), FRSA, Churchill Fellow

Eunice

The crop is local children
and though she's 83
she grows them sweet and bright and strong
and weans them off TV.

With spirit and with energy
this gardener took the lead
and in a small allotment
she planted a seed.

Local children come for fun
and learn to grow fresh food
and nothing here is wasted
all is used for good.

The garden feeds the children.
community prospers too.
SOB grew from the riots
troubled Handsworth had gone through

The first Booklet produced telling Eunice McGhie-Belgrave's Story with Ikon Gallery Staff.

Appendix 1

Appendix 2

Generation Windrush

In 2019, Mrs Eunice McGhie-Belgrave Belgrave MBE was featured in a documentary called "Generation Windrush".

This transcript from the film highlights the climate that Eunice and her family, along with thousands of migrants, faced.

1. We often talk about Caribbean people being 'invited' to work here, but secret government documents show that in private, the government did not want people from the Caribbean to come.

In 1948 when the possibility of using West Indian labour had been raised earlier in Cabinet, the Ministry of Labour had taken the position that…

"Caribbean workers were unsuitable for outdoor work owing to their susceptibility of cold and lung ailments".

But although they thought it was too cold, they also said the mines were **"too hot"** for Caribbean workers.

It asserted **"many of the coloured men are unreliable, lazy, and quarrels among them are not infrequent"**.

2. The government did not want the Windrush to land in Britain. As it was crossing the Atlantic, the Prime Minister enquired as to whether it could be prevented from docking and rerouted to East Africa. They feared 'coloured migration.'

On the very day it docked, June 22nd 1948, 11 MP's wrote a letter to the Prime Minister stating that;

"The British people enjoy a profound unity without uniformity and are blessed by the absence of a colour racial problem. An influx of coloured people domiciled here is likely to impair the harmony, strength and cohesion of our public and social life and to bring discord and unhappiness to all concerned… We venture to suggest the governmentGovernment should, by legislation if necessary, control immigration in the political, social, economic and fiscal interests of our people".

The response was that the **'problem'** was being **'vigorously dealt with'** and that **'every possible step had been taken to discourage these influxes'**.

3. In 1952 Winston Churchill wanted to stop Caribbean people from coming to Britain. So, he commissioned a reportReport on the "coloured people" currently living in Britain. Police forces in cities where there was a "coloured" population were asked to **"observe, visit and report on"** the black population to show their criminality.

When it was finished it also said, "coloured workers" were not good workers because of their **"low output... high rate of turnover... irresponsibility, quarrelsomeness and lack of discipline"**.

"Coloured women" were **"slow mentally"** and the men, **"more volatile in temperament than white workers... more easily provoked to violence... lacking in stamina"**.

4. The Report also offered further proof of Caribbean people's unsuitability to live in Britain by their **"primitive, squalid and deplorable"** living conditions.

5. To stop Caribbean people from coming, the plan was to create new laws. This was necessary, they said **"if there is to be any means of controlling the increased flow of coloured people who come here largely to enjoy the benefits of the Welfare State."**

6. The government admitted that **"if we legislate on immigration, though we can draft it in non-discriminatory terms, we cannot conceal the obvious fact that the object is to keep out coloured people."**

7. However, in 1955 the public were not as concerned with immigration as the government was. So, the government decided that it needed to **"educate public opinion on the subject"**.

They wanted to **"ensure that the public throughout the country were made aware of the nature and extent of the problem"** of Caribbean migration.

So, they formed a committee – it was called **"The Interdepartmental Working Party on the Social and Economic Problems Arising From the Growing Influx into the UK of Coloured Workers from Commonwealth Countries"**.

8. When they finally did manage to create legislation in 1962 that closed the door to Caribbean migrants, the Home Secretary said privately that theits **"great merit"** of their law was that it seemed non-discriminatory whereas **"its restrictive effect is intended to, and would in fact, operate on coloured people almost exclusively"**.

Add footnote _ report on coloured people

Appendix 3   Awards

1990	Sunday Mercury Care Medal Award
1994	Invitation to Buckingham Palacepala
	Maverick Mental Health Creative Sparkle Award
1996	Area Resident's' Association Squirrel Award
	TSB Adult Citizens Award
	Changing Taste of Food Black Workers' Community Award
2000	Invitation to St James's Palace
	The MBE Award
2001	Action Ministries International Award
2002	Two *Evening Mail* and Pallasades Local Heroes Awards
2003	Two The Institute of Jamaica Heroes Awards
2005	Two Local Lord Mayor's Awards
2011	WRVS Local Hero Awards
1997	Focus Mental Health House of Commons Award
2004	Two visits to St James's Palace to meet the Queen for Queen's Jubilee Awards
2005	Invitation to the Good Food Show
2009	Pride of Britain Award
2012/2013	Highgrove Prince Charles Garden Visit
2013	Organic Award
2016	Elders Award
2018	St George Silver Cross Award
	Lifetime Achievement Award
2019	Pride of Britain Award Featured

Appendix 4

Appendix 5

Television Appearances

BBC Gardeners World
Pride of Britain - ITV
Generation Windrush Channel 4

BBC Worldwide

BBC Worldwide Limited
Media Centre 2D1
201 Wood Lane
London W12 7TQ
bbcworldwide.com

22 December 2008

Dear Mrs McGhie Belgrave MBE

Thank you so much for your help and involvement in the making of our allotments feature on Shades of Black. Nick and Jane have told us how wonderful you have been. Enclosed is a dvd of the shots that Nick has kindly duplicated for us to send to you. We think they're great. Hope you like them too. We are also sending a copy to Joanne Wedderburn at Rookery School. If all goes according to plan Shades of Black will be featured in our June 2009 issue.

Wishing you a wonderful Christmas and a productive new year.

Best wishes

Abigail Dodd
Creative Director
BBC Gardeners' World magazine
020 8433 3962

From all the team at
Gardeners' World magazine

This card supports

Cancer Research UK, 61 Lincoln's Inn Fields, London WC2A 3PX
Tel. 020 7242 0200
www.cancerresearchuk.org

Reg Charity No. 1089464

Wishing you a Merry Christmas and a Happy New Year

I am now 85 years of Age and my work continues on in 2020

References and photograph credits

http://www.sobhelpproject.org.uk/

pintrest.com

Jamaica.com

Jamaica history weebly.com

JA.blogspot.com

3bp.blogspot.com

PoppyBrady The Voice Newspaper

Birmingham Library and Museum Services Archives

Pride of Britain ITV and The Mirror

Birmingham Mail

BBC Gardeners World

New Nation Newspaper

Uplands TV

Channel 4

To contact Mrs Eunice McGhie-Belgrave MBE
email info@marciampublishing.com

www.marciampublishing.com

Printed in Poland
by Amazon Fulfillment
Poland Sp. z o.o., Wrocław